Fictional Combat
Angela Knight's Guide to Writing Fight Scenes
Angela Knight

Fictional Combat
Angela Knight's Guide to Writing Fight Scenes
Angela Knight

All rights reserved.
Copyright ©2025 Angela Knight

ISBN: 978-1-60521- 934-9

Publisher:
Changeling Press LLC
315 N. Centre St.
Martinsburg, WV 25404
ChangelingPress.com

Printed in the U.S.A.

Editor: Jean Cooper
Cover Artist: Angela Knight

The individual stories in this anthology have been previously released in E-Book format.

Table of Contents

Fictional Combat
Angela Knight's Guide to Writing Fight Scenes
Angela Knight

As a novelist, teacher and editor, I've seen bad fight scenes ruin too many good stories. My objective in this book is to demonstrate how to write fights that keep readers on the edge of their seats -- and publishers begging for more.

I'll discuss how to use YouTube to research combat techniques and construct thrilling fights blow by blow. You'll also learn how to use those fights to reveal character and build reader sympathy.

I'll demonstrate the warning signs of an anticlimax and what to do about it. I'll show you how to build tension and excitement with every battle until you reach a climax that has the reader craving your next book.

Introduction

Knowing how to write an exciting fight scene is crucial in genres ranging from romance to horror. As a teacher and editor, I've seen bad fights ruin too many good stories.

My objective in this book is to share techniques that keep readers on the edge of their seats -- and publishers begging for more. You'll learn how to use YouTube to research combat techniques and construct thrilling sequences blow by blow. I'll also demonstrate how to use those scenes to reveal character and build reader sympathy. You'll learn what anticlimaxes are and how to avoid them. I'll also share the tricks of building reader tension with every fight until you reach an exhilarating climax that will make you an autobuy.

The Anti-romance
What do steamy love scenes and vicious brawls have in common?

In both combat and sex, two or more people use their bodies to express strong emotions. In one, it's the growing passion between a couple, while in the other, it's the growing hate between protagonist and antagonist.

The more anger and lethal determination you build into your anti-romance, the more your reader will enjoy the book.

Remember this formula:
High Emotion = High Drama and reader fascination.

Low Emotion = Low tension and reader boredom.

Why? Though we all like to see ourselves as

driven by reason and logic, our emotions are the real engine of our actions. The more intense your feelings about someone else, the more you're inclined to act on those feelings with a kiss -- or a slap.

Readers quickly become addicted to stories with strong conflicts inspired by strong emotions. But what causes that addiction, and how do you engineer your story to feed it?

Chapter One: The Fiction Addiction

Over almost three decades as a professional novelist, I've learned tons of useful storytelling tricks. Yet I haven't always understood *why* those tricks work. As a result, in the past I'd indulge in too much backstory or commit some other error that killed a scene's tension.

I did know good stories need a hook that pulls readers in. But turns out, what you really need isn't *one* hook, but the fictional equivalent of Velcro -- hundreds of tiny hooks the reader has no desire to escape. Fights -- and conflict in general -- make excellent Velcro.

I also learned which mistakes can do the opposite of hooking: *hurling* a reader right out of the story. I'll show you how to avoid them later.

Storytelling and the Brain

What do good books, college graduations, professional football, weddings, and chocolate have in common? As Lisa Cron points out in her terrific book, *Wired for Story* (Cron 2012), it's dopamine -- the brain chemical that rewards us for accomplishing something difficult.

Remember the rush when you graduated high school or college? That was dopamine. Your incandescent happiness at your wedding or the birth of your child? Dopamine. Even chocolate and cocaine trigger dopamine, the first a little of it, the latter a *lot*.

Dopamine floods can even be triggered by someone else's success. Remember your joy when your favorite team won the Super Bowl? You were just sitting on your couch, but you still felt as if you'd personally scored that winning touchdown.

The harder you work for something, the greater

the dopamine rush your brain produces when you succeed. Things you don't work as hard for -- say, a candy bar -- don't have the same payoff. As Cron points out, dopamine kept our cave-dwelling ancestors fighting to kill that tasty mastodon. Yeah, you might get stomped, but if you pulled it off, your tribe would eat for days.

Even today, it's hard to get motivated without dopamine (*Cognifit*, "New Study Redefines How Dopamine..." Dec. 26, 2024). That's why people with ADHD need drugs like Ritalin -- their brains just don't produce enough of the neurochemical to keep them on task.

Why does that matter to writers? When a character wins the climactic battle through hard, grinding work and painful effort, we experience a rush of dopamine as though it were *our* victory. Just like that winning touchdown you had nothing to do with.

But what if the protagonist's back is to the wall and she's gearing up for a fight to the death with her terrifying antagonist? And then...

...The bad guy gets hit by a bus.

"*No!*" the readers scream. They've empathized with the heroine, shared her dogged struggles, celebrated her victories, and suffered her defeats. They just knew the climax would deliver a tsunami of dopamine goodness. And *this* is all they get?

That's what an anticlimax is. For writers, it's like French-kissing death. Readers neither forget nor forgive an anticlimax.

Unfortunately, it's also a mistake common to newbie authors. The writer loves their heroine and doesn't want her to experience the terror and life-threatening injuries of a fight to the death. Empathy comes easily to writers -- that's what lets us imagine why and how other people suffer. Too, imagining a fight with a terrifying enemy is stressful.

Unwilling -- or lacking the confidence -- to plunge into the emotional storm of a thundering climax, the novelist goes easy on the protagonist.

Look, I get it. Like most people, I try to be a kind person in real life. But when my fingers hit the keyboard, I'm the biggest bitch in romance.

A good writer is a merciless god. Yet it's cruelty with a purpose, because it forces the protagonist to discover their strengths and overcome their fears. In sharing that struggle, the reader may experience more than just a happy buzz -- they may find the courage to face their own challenges. There have been times in my life that felt unbearably dark and grim, yet a novel helped me find the hope and guts to keep going. *"Hey, if a vampire who hates his own penis can overcome his self-loathing, maybe I've got a shot at it too."*

I genuinely believe giving other people courage is the best reason to be a writer. But to do so, you must be willing to put your characters through the hell of a hard, desperate fight.

I guarantee some of your readers are facing their own brutal challenges. Let them find hope -- and a welcome distraction -- in your fictional world.

Dances with Dopamine

It's the writer's job to construct conflicts so intense, the resulting climax sends readers sailing on an ocean of dopamine.

To do that, you must establish from the beginning that your protagonists face overwhelming odds. Yet they'll fight to their last breath because losing would exact a price they don't want to pay -- their future, their dreams, or the lives of people they love.

This tells the reader that: A) the resulting dopamine flood is going to be powerful because the conflict is so intense, and B) the protagonist won't give up and leave the reader seething with frustration because you got them all worked up for nothing.

We call it a climax for reason. Readers want us to get them off.

We seduce them by delivering a series of challenges that grow progressively more difficult. The characters must fight like hell until the climax sends the readers floating off on a surge of dopamine.

That's how you become an auto-buy.

We also get dopamine from other sources than winning a battle -- and they all make good hooks for your story. Dopamine triggers include:

- Surprise
- Humor
- Love scenes
- Collecting clues about where the story is going
- Solving a mystery
- Learning something new.

As Lisa Cron points out in *Story Genius* (Cron 2016), a good story also generates the stress hormone cortisol, which makes you worry about a character. That worry drives you to keep reading to make sure they're going to get out of their current mess.

Another terrific hormonal weapon in the writer's armory is oxytocin. Oxytocin causes that sweet, warm calm you get from hugs, the aftermath of an orgasm, or breastfeeding a baby. Romance readers crave that as much as dopamine. The more touches, hugs, kisses, and orgasms you describe throughout the book, the more little spurts of oxytocin the reader gets.

Using all three kinds of hormonal hooks ensures your reader won't be able to put the book down.

Talking About Fight Club

One of the bedrock commandments of the writing craft is, "Write what you know." Which can be a problem when it comes to combat. Most of us -- particularly women -- were last in a fight in tenth grade. Me writing a medieval melee is like a virgin writing erotic romance.

Luckily, I took fencing in college. It's been decades, but I still recall what I felt on the fencing strip: the intense concentration, the effort and exhaustion, the desire to avoid pain and defeat my opponent. (Getting hit with a foil -- the capped blade used in the sport -- leaves painful bruises the size of dimes.)

I've found I can apply that experience to the fights I write. Those matches would have been even more intense if we'd been using real swords.

You, too, may want to take a martial arts or boxing class to learn what combat feels like. You'd learn how to throw punches or kicks, experience the jarring sting as you block your opponent's blows or take a punch in the face. The effort, exhaustion, and ache will give you a visceral understanding of combat in a way nothing else can.

But if you can't take classes for physical or financial reasons, there are plenty of other ways to learn how people fight.

When I first decided I wanted to be a writer, I spent a lot of time in libraries reading up on martial arts and swordplay. Unfortunately, it's tough to visualize techniques from a book. It's far better to *see* someone demonstrate the move you're writing about.

That's why YouTube has become my go-to research solution when I'm working through a fight scene. I've found useful combat demonstrations by everyone from cops to martial artists to medieval reenactors. Even better, *it's all free*.

When I'm about to write a fight, I spend a day or two watching videos, looking for effective attacks and how to defend against them. I also note spectacular moves that would make a good fight-ending blow.

Next, I create a playlist of those videos to refer to during the writing process. That done, I write a list of the blows, blocks, and counter-attacks my characters would use, in order.

- Antagonist A tries to sucker punch Protagonist coming out of a bar.
- Protagonist pivots, dodging the blow, and punches A.
- A falls back against the wall, then lowers his head and charges, tackling Protagonist around the waist and knocking him to the ground.
- Protagonist blocks A's punch and head-butts him...

That list is the skeleton of the scene's choreography. It's easier to think thorough the logical sequence of the blows and blocks without the distraction of writing the scene.

With the skeleton done, I put meat and muscle on those bones. I imagine myself as the characters, feeling each blow or block -- the jarring punches, the stunning impact of a head-butt, trying to blink the tears away so you can defend yourself. The rage and desperation. What the setting looks, sounds, smells, and tastes like. Using lush descriptions helps the reader experience the scene, drawing them deeper into the story until they almost feel they *are* the characters. The protagonist's struggles, failures -- and victories -- become the reader's.

And that's exactly what you want.

My YouTube system has served me well even when writing some seriously weird fights, like *Master of Magic*'s battle between two griffins. (Knight 2017) A griffin is a mythical medieval beast which looks like a lion with the wings, forelegs, and head of an eagle. How would something like that fight? I'd already researched leonine combat for another book, but how would those attacks work in the air?

I headed to YouTube's many nature videos to learn how eagles fight. I'd assumed they'd use their talons and beaks to rend and bite, but nope. Turns out they dive at each other, lock their talons together in midair and whip in circles around their joined claws as they fall to the ground. The centripetal force rips at them until one bird loses its grip and sails off into defeat.

The video of the huge birds spinning as they fell was so striking, I knew I'd found the fight's climax. When writing a fight, you need a climactic blow the readers don't see coming. The unexpected triggers a dopamine buzz all by itself.

Eagles spinning through the air like ballroom dancers is damned unexpected.

On the other hand, grabbing claws doesn't sound particularly lethal, even if you're plummeting to the ground at the time. Fortunately, I had the lion half of the griffin to take up the slack. Lions often try to disembowel each other with their rear claws when they grapple. Combine grappling and disemboweling, and you've got a nice, vicious climax.

Choreographing Mayhem

I've found YouTube handy for researching everything from the art of tattooing to how Marines searched Afghan caves.

You can even find techniques you wouldn't expect to see demonstrated at all, like the swordplay practiced by medieval knights. The reenactors of HEMA -- short for Historical European Martial Arts -- recreate traditional fighting techniques. (HEMA practitioners determine that based on period combat manuals written for fighters of a given era.) If you're writing a novel featuring swordplay, YouTube's HEMA channels will teach you what you need to know.

For example, I was surprised to learn armored knights were much more agile than the lumbering human tanks depicted in film and television. One guy demonstrated the point by somersaulting like Simone Biles -- in *full plate armor*. Who knew?

If you want to learn how to do just about anything, whether it's replacing a blown fuse or carving an ice sculpture, YouTube is a great place to start. (Though you do have to watch out for scammers trying to sell you snake oil.)

Another source of combat inspiration are films and television with particularly dazzling choreography. When you find a fight exciting, watch the scene over and over, making use of the pause button to get a feel for the choreography. Analyze what made that scene so gripping and see if you can create similar effects.

One movie I found inspiring was 2017's *Atomic*

Blonde. Charlize Theron plays an American spy hunting double agents before the 1989 collapse of the Berlin Wall. That movie has some of the most brutal fights involving a female protagonist I've ever seen.

In one especially vicious sequence, the heroine and her male opponent periodically break off and collapse, panting and glaring, until they regain the strength to go at each other again. This made the film seem more realistic and heightened the sense of danger.

Then there's *Quantum of Solace*, staring Daniel Craig as James Bond. You don't find much dialogue in the Craig brawls, unlike some of the campy sequences from the older Bond films. His battles all have a raw savagery that catapults your heart into your throat. The camera work is so jerky and chaotic that it gives you a sense of what it must be like to fight for your life.

A good fight reveals character. Craig's Bond is a ruthless man who doesn't let fear or pain stop him. He is powerful, agile, and highly skilled, as well as insanely brave and dedicated to serving his country.

Which brings me to my next topic: characterization.

It's said you never really know someone until you see them in danger. What will they do when their lives are on the line? Will they fight or run? Will they risk their lives for the people they love?

A protagonist can talk a good game all they want, but readers won't believe they're heroic until they prove it. Too, there is no better way to build sympathy for a character than to show them fighting for survival.

Chapter Two: Heart and the Warrior

Readers care about the outcome of a fight only if they're deeply invested in one of the fighters. That's why characterization is key.

Humans are social animals. We're fascinated by other people and want to know what drives them. Take the public's obsession with celebrities. We see actors or singers in film or on television, and we hunger to know more about them. Why do they do what they do? What are their lives like? The media satisfies that curiosity with gossip about their children, marriages, affairs, and divorces, creating the illusion of intimacy.

Books are even better at creating intimacy, since no camera can show what's going on inside someone's head. Your job is to engineer characters who seem so real, readers feel they know them -- and even *become* them.

Make Me Care

We care about the fates of our friends and enemies. We want to see them happy or get their comeuppance. We cheer for them or root for their downfall.

But there are billions of people on this planet, and you can't care about everybody. You've probably experienced this in your own life, especially on plane flights. Remember when the stranger sitting next to you started telling you all about their bum knee? Even as you nodded politely, you thought, *I don't care. I just want to take a nap.*

Fictional people can be a lot like that if the writer isn't careful.

I often judge writing contests. One entry

included the kind of stuff I normally enjoy -- vampires and shapeshifters having lots of hot sex. Unfortunately, getting laid was the characters' only goal. Why should I care whether those people had an orgasm? The author didn't give me *the* reason to become invested in them: a good problem.

An effective story problem has consequences that could change the protagonist's life for the worse. High stakes pull the reader in. I don't just mean death, but job loss, social or financial ruin, or rejection by someone you love.

If you don't get laid, what happens? Despite what teenage boys believe, nobody ever died from blue balls. Even if you *do* get sex, what happens? Orgasms are nice, but they don't change your life. (Unless you fall in love with your sex partner.)

Think of it this way: would you be fascinated by a book about somebody getting takeout pizza? I doubt it. Now, I might care if the protagonist has just escaped a serial killer, is dying of starvation, and is flat broke. Otherwise, Joe Blow on a pizza run does *not* make my heart pound.

What does this tell us about creating characters?

A good character needs something badly -- and will suffer if they don't get it. To heighten reader interest, give them an antagonist who needs the opposite and will suffer just as much if they fail to get it.

No matter who wins, *somebody's* going to suffer.

Keep this formula in mind: **Need + Obstacle = Conflict**. Take away either the need or the obstacle, and you've got no conflict -- and no story.

The Ins and Outs of Conflict

In fiction, there are two types of conflict: *internal*

and *external*.

External conflict comes from *outside* the character -- from other people, nature or society. Bad guy vs. good guy is an example of an external conflict. So are romantic conflicts.

Internal conflict takes place *inside* the character's head. These conflicts often begin with some kind of trauma -- fear of fire, PTSD, an abusive lover who has left the character with a psychic wound, etc. The wound can also result from something less dire, such as a lack of self-confidence from parents who spent the character's childhood denigrating them.

The character develops a strategy to protect them from future wounds. Let's say your protagonist was in a horrible car crash, so trying to drive triggers panic attacks. Eventually she quits driving completely.

Being a sadistic bitch, I'd put her in a situation where her ex hurts her child so badly, the little boy is bleeding to death. The 911 dispatcher tells her all the ambulances are tied up with a 50-car pileup on the Interstate. She must drive her son to the hospital herself.

Dealing with an injured child is traumatic enough. Fighting a phobia on top of that would make the situation unbearable.

If the external conflict -- the injured child -- can't be solved because of the coping strategy -- never driving -- the result is a brutal internal conflict.

If the ex is chasing them with intent to murder them both, defeating him becomes even harder. She can succeed only when she realizes how toxic her strategy is, overcomes her phobia, and *drives*.

Readers love internal conflicts because they make everything harder. And that equals more dopamine in the climax.

If you've ever been told your protagonist is two-dimensional, it's probably because they lack a strong internal conflict. Every real-life human is screwed up over *something*, so a perfectly well-adjusted protagonist isn't realistic. Worse, they may be boring.

You want to set up a situation in which the internal and external conflict grind against each other (as in my phobic mother example above) until the protagonist overcomes their psychic wound.

That's why every time I create a protagonist, the first question I ask is, "How and why is this person screwed up?"

A strong internal conflict makes a character more unpredictable -- and therefore more interesting. Say your war hero protagonist wants to save a child from a burning building. But what if he suffered third-degree burns in combat, and PTSD threatens to freeze him in his tracks? What will he do then? Even *he* doesn't know. That uncertainty makes the scene more exciting because he's fighting himself as much as the fire.

Next, design an external conflict that triggers the character's internal conflict. For instance, in the burning building example, I'd make the antagonist an arsonist who has been hired to kill the child to teach her parents a lesson. A set of tightly interlocking conflicts make readers wonder how the protagonist can possibly survive. They'll keep reading to find out.

Romantic Conflict

Romantic conflicts are a type of external conflict in that they originate *outside* the character. The romantic conflict is the reason the heroic couple believes they won't end up together, no matter how sexually attracted they are.

If you're writing science fiction, horror,

espionage, etc., a romance may be a simple subplot. In that case, the romantic conflict doesn't have to be that powerful, since love isn't the focus of the book.

But if you're writing a romance, the couple's relationship *is* the focus -- the oxytocin source the reader craves. But just as in fight scenes, you can't make a Happy Ever After (HEA) look too easy. A weak romantic conflict equals a weak romance, no matter how hot the sex or menacing the villain. Romantic conflict is the engine of the book, acting to drive the lovers apart and make a Happily Ever After appear impossible.

(In a romance, the antagonist often acts as a matchmaker, forcing the couple to work together when the romantic conflict would otherwise drive them apart. Which adds to the unpredictability of the story. Dopamine!)

Note that when I say, "a good romantic conflict," I'm not talking about stupid misunderstandings. (If the words "she's my sister" can resolve it, it's a lousy conflict.) What you want is something born of *who the characters are*. (Say, vampire and vampire hunter.) You must make the reader doubt a HEA is even in the cards. Without a strong romantic conflict, there's zero tension, which will kill your book every time.

Let's look at how to establish your book's conflicts while making your reader care about your protagonists.

Designing Women (And Men)

In *Master of Fire* (Knight 2010), antagonist Terrance John Anderson has been hired to kill my hero, Logan MacRoy. (He soon discovers that the werewolves who hired him will punish him in horrific ways if he fails.) Logan, of course, will die if he can't fend the villain off. My heroine, Giada Shepherd, has been sent to protect Logan. None of the three can afford to lose.

Master of Fire is the sixth book in my *Mageverse* series, in which King Arthur and the Knights of the Round Table are vampires and their ladies are immortal witches. Collectively, they're called the Magekind, and they're all sworn to protect humanity.

In the world of the Magekind, you don't become a vampire by being bitten, but by having sex three times with a Maja (a witch.) This triggers Merlin's Gift, a spell passed down in the DNA of the Magekind's mortal descendants.

The romantic conflict in *Master of Fire* is that Logan, Arthur's son, does not want to become a vampire. He plans to stay mortal and work for a South Carolina sheriff's office as a forensic chemist and bomb disposal expert.

He doesn't know a gang of werewolves is methodically murdering descendants of the Magekind. As Arthur's son, Logan is a prime target.

Arthur sends Giada Shepherd to protect him, so she gets a job with the sheriff's office as a forensic chemist. (She earned a doctorate in chemistry before becoming a witch.) Arthur orders her to keep his son in the dark, since he thinks Logan won't allow her to stick close if he learns she's a Maja. He also warns her not to get emotionally involved or sleep with Logan. Arthur doesn't want his son to think he's trying to trick him into becoming a vampire.

Giada's internal wound is a stubborn sense of inferiority because she's not very powerful as witches go. Since she was a prodigy as a child, she hates feeling like a failure as a witch. This hits her particularly hard because she went to college at fourteen. She lacks the sexual experience and romantic confidence you get from dating and socializing with peers. No matter what her mirror tells her, inside she's still the chubby, too-smart nerd who never fit in. She's determined to prove herself to Arthur and the rest of the Magekind.

Logan's internal conflict -- the reason he doesn't want to become a vampire -- is that the transformation spell can drive people insane. The Magekind must then kill the rogue to keep them from going on a killing spree. Arthur has had to slay one son already -- the treacherous Mordred, who led a rebellion against him fifteen centuries before. Logan fears that being forced to kill him too would destroy the father he worships.

You can see how all these people are at cross purposes. There are potent consequences to failure, so nobody can just give up and go home.

Capturing reader interest

I spent a lot of time working out the conflicts for *Master of Fire* and deciding how they'd play out. Once I had the plot, I had to write a dynamite first scene to introduce the characters and lay out the conflicts without boring the crap out of people. That's critical, since the first chapter is the hook that pulls in your readers -- and your potential publisher.

You need an incident that makes readers care about the protagonists. Early chapters should also establish the antagonist as a menace so readers will worry about your heroes.

You don't have to show both the protagonists and antagonists in the same first scene, but you should introduce everyone as soon as you can. Create a sense of rising jeopardy so that the reader knows things are going to get exciting fast.

And you must do it without a backstory dump. For

one thing, a data dump answers all the reader's questions, denying them the dopamine from asking questions and gathering clues about what's going on.

The trick is to judge precisely how much the reader needs to know to follow the action. Confusing the hell out of them will send them sailing out of the book. That can be a hard trap to avoid. As the writer, you've spent a lot of time developing these people and the world they live in, and your impulse is to tell the reader everything.

Don't.

In my early books, I often had ten-page prologue data dumps. Since then, I've realized readers hate having a brick of backstory shoved down their throats. They'll choke every time.

How much should you tell readers? *As little as possible.* No more than a sentence here, a paragraph there. And those paragraphs should *not* be in the first chapter. The more questions you can make readers ask about what's going on in the first chapter, the better off you are. Curiosity will keep them reading in search of a lovely little dopamine buzz as they make predictions and find out if they're right.

Here's how I set up my hero, heroine, and villain in *Master of Fire*, along with notes to explain the techniques I use.

> The truck bounced down the snaking gravel driveway that led to the dead man's house. (*A good first sentence is a hook all by itself, making the reader wonder, "What the hell is going on here? Why is this truck going to a dead man's house?" The idea is to make the reader read on to find out more*).
>
> It was a huge armored box of a vehicle, gleaming

black, with "Bucks County Sheriff's Office Bomb Disposal Team" painted on the side in white lettering. (*So not only is it a truck going to a dead man's house, it's a* bomb *truck going to a dead man's house.*)

Terrence John Anderson watched through his binoculars as the truck rolled up to the old white farmhouse. He lay hidden in a leafy clump of bushes at the edge of the woods, camouflage paint smearing his face, ice gray eyes narrow and watchful amid the writhing patterns of green and black. A sniper rifle lay beside him, but it was just for insurance. (*Note the menacing phrases "ice gray eyes," and "writhing patterns of green and black." From the first scene, you want your reader to worry about what the antagonist is going to do. Keep in mind that romance readers often assume the first male they encounter is the hero. You don't want them to mistake the antagonist for your lead. Making him sound creepy does the job.*)

He had something more dramatic in mind than a bullet. (By now the reader should be wondering who Terrance is planning to kill and how he's planning to do it.)

Now to introduce my heroine.

The truck rolled to a stop, and a woman climbed out of the passenger side. He focused the binocs on her. Tall, dressed in wide-legged navy pants that swirled around her long legs. A flowing pale blue blouse draped over lush breasts and nipped in around her narrow waist, cinched by a wide navy belt. Her blonde hair was pulled into a twist on the back of her head, but the severe hairstyle only emphasized the lush beauty of her mouth, the size of her eyes, the line of her nose. Even at this distance, she was stunning.

She scanned the area, her expression watchful and wary. He wondered how she'd look after the bomb got done with that pretty face. (*There's a bomb here somewhere, but where? And obviously, she knows there's something bad going on -- she's not just a helpless victim. This tells us she's the heroine.*)

Almost a shame, really. (*The antagonist feels no sense of regret or doubt about what he's going to do to this poor woman.*)

Lt. Logan MacRoy walked around the side of the truck to join the blonde. He was a big man, broad-shouldered in the black knit shirt of the bomb squad, with his military-style uniform pants tucked into combat boots. Terrence felt his muscles coil in anticipation. His sheriff's department contact had been right. The e-mail from i4ni@zoom.com had said MacRoy was the bomb squad tech on call today. Sure enough, here he was.

Terrence did love a reliable informant. (*So now we know there's a traitor in the sheriff's office that our protagonists don't know about. The situation keeps getting more and more complicated -- which is just how readers like it.*)

The file the client had provided said MacRoy was thirty-one years old, six-foot-four, two-hundred-twenty pounds, Caucasian, brown and brown. A lieutenant with the Bucks County Sheriff's Office, he'd graduated at the top of his class at the South Carolina law enforcement academy. No surprise, considering he also had a master's degree in chemistry. (*This paragraph is a bit of a data dump, but I can get away with it because I've already set my hooks. Readers will just suck up all this information, looking for clues for their dopamine hunt.*)

MacRoy had a long list of other certifications as well, including arson investigator and, of course, bomb squad tech. An unusual set of qualifications for a forensic chemist, according to Terrence's research. (*This tells you that Logan saves people's lives for a living, which will help make the reader more invested in him.*)

Actually, it was pretty rare for a southern sheriff's office to have a lab at all; those that did kept their chemists busy testing seized cocaine, pot, crack and methamphetamine. Logan had evidently talked his sheriff into letting him do a lot more, maybe on the strength of his nine years in law enforcement. He'd been one of the first sheriff's department forensic chemists in South Carolina. (*Establishes where we are. You always need to make sure the reader knows where and when the story takes place.*)

Somewhere along the line, he'd also pissed somebody off. Really, really bad. Terrence John Anderson bad. (*After three paragraphs of data dump, I need to remind the reader that Bad Stuff Is Going to Happen. Now, I wrote* Master of Fire *years ago. Today I'd probably cut most of this, because I don't think we need to know it all.*)

Terrence lifted his cell phone and thumbed 119.

Listened to the beep that signaled his booby-trap was armed. And smiled in anticipation.

The blonde's head snapped up as if she'd somehow heard that tiny beep. She stared into the woods, right at Terrence, eyes narrow. (*My heroine is not just an ordinary woman with ordinary senses.*)

The assassin froze, except for the slight movement of his hand finding the rifle. He could snatch it up and fire before the little bitch got a shout of warning out of her mouth.

The metal bracelet the client had given him suddenly blazed hot around his wrist, a ferocious burning bite so intense he could almost smell his skin sizzle. He bit back a snarled curse. The blonde's gaze turned uncertain, and she scanned the woods around him in confusion. (*This is a plot hole plug. Since Giada is a witch, she should find the guy right off, so I had the boss villain give him a magical bracelet that blocks her abilities. This also makes the reader wonder just who his client is, and why he wants Logan dead.*)

And then she looked away.

The pounding of his heart began to slow, and his hand slid away from the rifle. Seems she hadn't seen him after all.

He could let the chemist go find his little surprise. (*Now I must make the reader care about my couple. I've established that they're in danger, which can be enough all by itself, but I also need to show that they're decent people who don't deserve to die.*)

"Something wrong?" Logan asked in his deep

rumble of a voice.

Giada Shepherd wiped the wary frown off her face and turned toward him. "Thought I saw something moving in the woods." She shrugged and lied. "Just a squirrel."

She wasn't sure what it had been, but it hadn't been a squirrel. Overactive bodyguard imagination, maybe. Furry and four-legged, no.

But for a moment there, she'd felt such a sense of chill menace, she'd been unable to breathe. Then it was just gone. Had to be her imagination, especially since she'd done a scanning spell and found nothing. (*Since I've shown the bracelet, I have to show its effect from her point of view to show it blocks her powers. We don't know how it works, and we're wondering who gave it to the antagonist and why.*)

On the other hand, it was daylight, and her magic wasn't all that reliable when the sun was up. Maybe somebody in those woods was eyeing Logan MacRoy's handsome head through a sniper scope. (*This point about her powers being limited in daylight is important to the scene that follows. Also, I'm showing the reader that this is a world in which magic works, and the heroine can cast spells.*)

That thought sent ice creeping down her spine on sharp little claws. She had to protect Logan. That was the whole point of this charade. (*She's willing to protect Logan from a psychotic bomber, even at risk to her own life. This also plays against stereotype since the man is usually the bodyguard, not the woman. To make things more interesting, Logan doesn't know he's being guarded. Plus, Giada is lying like hell to him.*)

Gravel crunched with the sound of running feet. Giada wheeled, only to relax as a little boy darted around the bulk of the bomb truck, his eyes wide as an anime character's under a mop of fine blond hair. She was no expert when it came to judging a child's age, but she figured he was no more than six or so.

He slid to a stop to study Logan with breathless excitement. "Are you a real cop?" His blue gaze darted to the weapons belt with its nine-millimeter automatic and handcuffs. "Is that a real gun?"

"Yep, and yep." Logan dropped to one black-clad knee and offered the kid a handshake, his smile broad and easy in a way Giada could only envy. She had never been that comfortable with children. *Probably because I never was one.* (*This paragraph does two things: it establishes that Logan is a nice, patient guy who likes children and is willing to take the time to talk to them, and it establishes that Giada is uncomfortable with kids. And what does she mean when she says she was never a child?*)

Her shoulder blades started itching again. She threw another look at the woods. It was getting a little too close to nightfall, and the trees swayed in a spring breeze, whispering secrets to the shadows.

Somebody out there might be getting ready to blow Logan's head off.

"Can we get this show on the road?" Giada demanded, interrupting Logan's earnest discussion of cop stuff with the kid. "It's been a long day, and I'd like to get back to my hotel."

Logan shot her a cool, disapproving look. Her cheeks heated.

She really hated sounding like such a bitch, but he didn't know the situation. And she couldn't tell him what was going on, or his mother would turn her into a frog. (*Okay, so who's his mother, and why and how would she turn Giada into a frog?*)

Or not. Maybe the woman had been joking. On the other hand, Giada had no desire to spend the rest of her life cooling her ass on a lily pad. Like it or not, she had to keep MacRoy in the dark and feed him nothing but bullshit. (*Her internal conflict is that her orders require her to lie to Logan, and she doesn't like it. I also introduce some romantic conflict with his flare of disapproval. You need to make clear the romance isn't going to be smooth sailing.*)

* * *

In the space of five pages or so, I've laid out who everybody is and set my hooks to keep the reader reading. I've also established the problem and Giada's stakes if she fails her assignment -- Logan and the child could die.

This is a lot to do in a few pages, but if you sit and think about it long enough, you can come up with the perfect scene to establish your people and get readers excited about the ride to come.

One of the techniques I use to accomplish this is point of view. Anderson knows things Giada doesn't -- the fact that he's planted a bomb -- while Giada knows things he doesn't -- that she's a witch sent to protect Logan.

These conflicting points of view enhance interest

as readers try to predict what will happen next.

Unfortunately, point of view is trickier than it sounds.

Chapter Three: Whose Head is This Anyway?

Point of view depicts the sights, smells, tastes, sounds and emotions the viewpoint character experiences. Done well, it immerses readers in the scene so thoroughly, they don't even notice it. Since point of view (POV) is almost invisible, many new writers don't understand what it is or how to use it. Yet handling viewpoint well is critical to pulling readers into the story.

There's a gimmick sometimes used in television mysteries when they don't want to show the identity of the killer. The camera is positioned as if it's looking out of the villain's eyes. You can see the knife they're holding and the victim they attack, but you can't see the killer's face, any more than you can see your own without a mirror.

That's point of view. You're in the character's head, experiencing the scene, thinking their thoughts, feeling their sensations.

Head Hopping Headaches

Most writing teachers will tell you not to switch POV in the same scene, a mistake called *head hopping*. Editors consider it a deadly sin and the mark of an amateur.

To understand why, let's go back to our knife-wielding television killer. Imagine that the bad guy is in a fight with other bad guys, all armed with knives. Now imagine that in every shot, the camera switches to the POV of a different killer. One minute you're swinging the knife, the next it's coming at your chest. The next minute, you're in someone else's head in an entirely different fight.

To my knowledge, no one has ever done a scene

like that, probably because it would confuse the hell out of the audience. Viewers would have no idea who was doing what to whom.

Readers have the same problem when you head hop. It throws them completely out of the scene as they try to figure out whose viewpoint you're in. Anytime readers must reread to figure out what's going on, you've lost them. Confuse them too much, and they'll just stop reading.

Yet POV switches are necessary when you switch scenes, or to fulfill some other story demand.

Pulling Off POV Switches in a Fight (Or anywhere else.)

Let's say you have two characters fighting. Usually, you'd want to stay in the protagonist's viewpoint, but you might do a POV switch to build tension.

Let's say the first half of the scene is Gabriel's POV, but you want to show John's. Skip a line and start the first sentence of the new viewpoint with something like, "John snarled as Gabriel's knife scored his ribs. It stung like a bitch." By using John's name and the sensation he feels, we establish whose POV we're in. (Avoid clunky sentence structures like "It stung like a bitch, John thought." "*John thought*" is redundant because it's obvious we're in his viewpoint.)

Really, you don't even need the skipped line. Making the switch with a new paragraph is fine. But in both cases, you absolutely *must* start with the character's name and a sensation that shows we're now in their head.

If the line was simply, "John snarled," the reader will assume we're still in Gabriel's POV, and he saw John snarl. But by adding a sensation and a thought, we clarify we've switched heads. "John snarled at the cold rake of steel over his ribs. *Dammit, that hurts!*"

However, there are nuances to skillful POV use.

Let's get back to John and his ribs. "John snarled at the cold rake of steel over his ribs. *God, it hurts!* John's brawny pectorals flexed as he reddened in rage and pain."

If you're in John's head, he can't see himself redden. You've just jumped cameras again, changing POV in the same paragraph. Now your verbal "camera" is located outside John's body, as if you're watching John instead of *being* John.

The solution is to show John feeling the *sensations* of a flush. "John felt his cheeks heat with rage." That tells the reader he flushed without jumping POVs.

Also, watch the language you use in John's POV. The line, "John's brawny pectorals flexed" is out of character, because John probably doesn't think of his own pecs as "brawny."

When you're in deep POV, stick to the language and thoughts the character would use. John is not going to think about Gabriel being broad-shouldered and sexy, because the bastard is trying to kill him. Broad-shouldered and sexy is how the *writer* sees Gabriel, making that line *authorial intrusion* -- the author inserting their own opinion instead of the viewpoint character's. You must avoid reminding the reader you're making the whole thing up.

But as important as POV is, what readers are ultimately interested in is the characters' relationships with each other.

And that includes the anti-romance between the protagonist and the villain.

Chapter Four: The Anti-romance

A few bad men -- and women.

When you're creating your characters, you need to pay particular attention to the relationships between them. In a romance, the relationship between the book's lovers forms the story's heart. In a military or law enforcement novel, the friendships between teammates add emotional weight as they fight to survive and achieve their mission objective. Basically, they become each others' stakes.

But if you're writing something with a strong action component, you need to give every bit as much thought to the relationship between the protagonist and the antagonist. The hate between them must be just as intense as the love or friendship between your protagonists.

The antipathy may not start out intense -- but then, neither does love in a romance. Good fictional relationships grow and evolve as the characters get to know each other.

Just as a romance novelist tailors the hero and heroine for each other, you need to design your villain with your protagonist in mind. I often think of the bad guy as the good guy's reflection in a dark, distorted mirror.

For example, in *Master of Fire*, my cop hero and witch heroine are motivated by a strong sense of duty and concern for others. My villain is a hired assassin, a sociopath who gets a sense of power from blowing people up.

When the book begins, the bomber sees killing the hero as nothing more than fulfilling a contract. If he'd kept that attitude all the way through the book, whether he won or lost wouldn't mean anything more to him than a paycheck.

But when Giada and Logan keep surviving his best efforts to kill them, Terrence's ego is offended. His sense of power depends on people dying. If his bombs fail to kill his targets, his self-image and reputation will suffer.

That's why he gets really, really pissed. Because he's pissed, we see him start fantasizing about watching Logan and Giada die. I even considered having him masturbate to those fantasies because it would make the whole thing even creepier. Someone who finds eroticism in a violent act that is not innately sexual is more frightening than a mere killer. It makes the villain alien and terrifying.

Why did I go out of my way to make the antagonist so creepy? Because Giada is a witch, Logan becomes a vampire, and Terrence is a plain vanilla human. In any straight fight, those two would clean his clock. (I eventually compensate for this by giving Terrance reinforcements in the form of two psychopathic werewolves.)

A 98-pound weakling is *not* the guy you want to pit against your hero.

Take Superman and Lex Luthor. Without Kryptonite, Lex could never be a genuine threat to a man who can bounce bullets off his eyeballs. But whenever Kryptonite strips Clark of his invulnerability, strength, and speed, the stakes snap from non-existent to his possible death.

No stakes for the protagonist = a boring story for the reader.

The villain must appear to have an overwhelming advantage in any conflict with the protagonist. Either:

- The antagonist is more powerful physically,

magically, or in terms of wealth, status and influence.

- The protagonist doesn't know who the villain is so the Big Bad can strike from hiding.
- The antagonist has an army at their command.
- The antagonist knows the protagonist's weak spots and can exploit them.

Whatever kind of power the villain has, it must appear the protagonists don't have a prayer against him.

Take the Joker in Christopher Nolan's *The Dark Knight* (2008). The Joker is physically inferior to Batman, which is *not* something you usually want. We know right up front that if Bruce ever gets his hands on him, the Joker is screwed. Indeed, Batman beats the crap out of him several times.

Yet the Joker's real power comes from his madness and unpredictability. The fact that he seems to want Batman to kill him makes him that much more frightening. Sane, normal people don't enjoy real life pain and humiliation. (Sex games are another matter.)

The Joker is not normal, and he is not sane.

We also fear him because he strikes not at Batman, but at those Bruce cares about, like his girlfriend, cop allies, and innocent civilians. The Joker constructs a situation that forces Batman to choose between his secret identity and the lives of those he's sworn to protect.

Why not simply kill him? That's the Joker's genius. He realizes Batman's entire identity is built around protecting the people of Gotham. Bruce's parents had no protector when they were gunned down when he was a child, so he's determined no other child will ever suffer the same fate.

That's why *The Dark Knight* is an antiromance. Both men become obsessed with each other. The Joker even tells Batman, "You complete me," a line straight out of a Tom Cruise romance. But *The Dark Knight* is about more than exchanging punches. Its furious energy comes from Joker's weaponizing Bruce's greatest vulnerability: his sense of duty to the people of Gotham.

You can have any antagonist use the same dynamic against a protagonist driven by duty, from cops to Navy SEALs to vampire knights of the Round Table. Or, for that matter, a kindergarten teacher trying to protect her four-year-olds from a school shooter.

Our job as writers is to create the perfect villain to sense and attack our protagonist's greatest vulnerability.

- In a romance, that vulnerability is the lovers' passion for each other.
- In a mystery, it's the detective's devotion to justice.
- In a military adventure novel, it's the loyalty and friendship the team shares.

Let's look at two famous examples. In Shakespeare's *Othello*, Othello is a heroic man of action whom Iago goads into murdering his innocent wife. In *Hamlet*, Hamlet hesitates to kill Claudius because he can't decide whether it's the right thing to do. Basically, Hamlet thinks too much, while Othello thinks too little.

Had Hamlet faced Iago, he would have seen right through him. Had Othello faced Claudius, he'd have killed him in Scene II, avoiding much of *Hamlet's* body count. Both tragedies work because the villains turn the protagonists' strengths into weaknesses.

That's the key to writing a book that fascinates and absorbs readers: find the heroic core of your characters and create someone who can use it against them.

It takes thought and planning to craft the perfect villain for the protagonist's weak spot. The effort is worth it, though, because it's much easier to write a book with strong conflicts.

Weak villains create headaches because you must come up with ways to compensate for their weakness. Skilled, formidable antagonists make your life easier.

Chapter Five: Love Hurts

Writers must create situations that spawn conflicts the way a cat gives birth to a litter of kittens. Let me show you how I did that with *Master of Honor* (2020). Then I'll dissect its climactic fight for you.

Master of Honor, like *Master of Fire*, is set in the Mageverse, the magical universe where Arthur and his agents live. Our own universe has no magic, so they must draw on the Mageverse to work spells here. My witches create dimensional gates to travel back and forth between the two universes.

The book's hero is Ulf, one of the Knights of the Round Table, who falls in love with a mortal woman named Cheryl Parker in the early 1980s. They have a child, Adam, and live together happily for eleven years. Trouble arises when a Maja seer tells Ulf if he reveals who and what he is, it will result in a catastrophe that will destroy humanity.

The whole time they're together, he has to lie to Cheryl.

To make matters worse, my vampires fall into a coma at dawn. Every time his family starts asking questions about his fangs and weird behavior, he must have a Maja cast a spell to make them ignore his vampyness. Since a long-term mental spell is bad for the brain, Arthur finally tells him to leave them. He's guilt-ridden and crushed, but he knows his liege is right and walks out. Cheryl and ten-year-old Adam are devastated.

Why did I do all that? To create a set of ugly external, internal, and romantic conflicts that make the relationships between Ulf and his family radioactive. Yet I also need my readers to understand Ulf has good reasons for what he's done: he really does love his family. I don't want the reader chanting "Run away! Run away!" at Cheryl every time they make love.

This internal conflict catches Ulf in an agonizing emotional bear trap. And it doesn't do great things for Adam and Cheryl either. She becomes a nurse and never marries, and Adam grows up and goes to work as a television news videographer.

Which is how Ulf's son ends up on the scene in *Master of Fate* (2019) when the Magekind battle invading aliens called the Fomorians. Adam shoots live video of the Times Square fight and outs Arthur and the Magekind on live TV.

Oops.

Why did I do that? Because I needed to give the series a new direction so I could find new plot avenues to explore. I was getting stale, which happens when you write the same series for twenty years.

The Magekind decide to recruit Adam because of a Maja seer's vision that he's needed. In the following book, *Master of Passion* (2019), Ulf and a Maja named Opal are sent to transform Adam into a vampire. He agrees, though he's mad as hell at his father for keeping him and his mother in the dark. Despite his parents' lousy example, Adam and Opal end up falling in love in *Master of Passion*.

That book was an exploration of the damage a father can do to a son without meaning to, and how he seeks forgiveness. I really enjoyed writing *Master of Passion* but found myself wanting to give Ulf and Cheryl a happy ending too.

The problem was, Cheryl is sixty and mortal, and the immortal Ulf will inevitably outlive her. How could I get an HEA out of that? Especially since Ulf has lied like a serial killer and Cheryl's deeply wounded by those lies.

Mmmm. Conflict! Yummy, yummy conflict. How do I spawn even more conflict from that pregnant mama cat of rage, pain and betrayal?

Plus, I'd just spent four books playing with the Fomorians, and I'd killed off my Big Bad Fomorian king. I needed a different Bad who was even Bigger. I spent several weeks being blocked on the climax of *Master of Passion* before I came up with one.

It was time for a brush with mass extinction.

The surviving Fomorians kidnap Cheryl, demanding a ring Merlin gave Ulf fifteen hundred years before. The Fomorian queen knows the ring is the key to incredible power. What she *doesn't* know is that signet is part of a plan hatched by Merlin and a dying alien creature named Gaia.

Centuries before, Gaia and her people had fallen victim to a race of creatures called the Hive, which feed on life force. Merlin showed up and transferred the dying Gaia's spirit into the ring. He'd had a vision the Hive would attack Earth in the twenty-first century and wipe out all life.

Ulf doesn't know any of this because the Magekind can't sense the ring's magic and think it's inert.

The ring appearing inert patched a plot hole. How did Ulf wear that signet for fifteen centuries without anyone noticing all that boiling magic? But if the power came from another universe entirely, it would make sense that the Majae couldn't sense it. (This is part of the reason I was blocked. You must hang something like that on a logical hook or you'll break the reader's willingness to go along with it.) That alien magic would also explain why Gaia possesses Cheryl instead of one of the powerful witches standing around -- the spirit's magic is incompatible with theirs.

The advantage of that is that Ulf has been wearing the ring for 1,500 years, so Gaia knows everything he's seen and done in that time. She's even absorbed his fighting skills and experience, which she implants in Cheryl.

This patches yet another hole: how does a sixty-year-old nurse become Wonder Woman? (Gaia also magically enhances Cheryl's strength so she can use Ulf's skills, making her immortal so she looks twenty. Which is good because Ulf, being a vampire, looks about twenty himself.)

Now, other than wish fulfillment, what's the point of doing all that? The theme of the book is how a couple learns to forgive each other, despite the anger and pain that accretes in any long marriage. Ulf betrayed the hell out of Cheryl, though not with other women. She doesn't even know his real name, since he tells her his name is Paul Rogers. Ulf lies to the woman he loved for eleven years, explaining his frequent absences on missions by claiming he's a businessman who travels for work. And when push comes to shove, he keeps choosing his loyalty to Arthur over his loyalty to her. *Master of Honor* is about his character arc to finally choosing Cheryl.

But to have a really good romantic conflict, Ulf needs a reason to distrust Cheryl too. Gaia gives him one when she possesses Cheryl. He's afraid the spirit has wiped her mind and effectively killed her. Arthur's not thrilled about the situation either, since Cheryl is now more powerful than any of his witches.

Their suspicions grow in *Master of Honor*'s inciting incident. A dragon tries to burn a North Carolina town to the ground -- and the beast's magic looks just like Cheryl's. (The dragon is really a shapeshifting advance scout for the Hive, as Merlin and Gaia foresaw fifteen centuries before.)

Master of Honor's Internal, External and Romantic Conflicts

Cheryl's internal conflict is that just weeks ago she was an aging, perfectly ordinary nurse still in love with the man who'd walked out on her. Now a powerful alien spirit shares her mind, giving her immortality and enough power to stand toe-to-toe with the Magekind. But it comes at a price: she must fight and kill the Hivemother and her entire species before they wipe out humanity. Yet the closest Nurse Cheryl has ever come to physical combat is wrestling with violent patients.

Fortunately, Gaia's given her all Ulf's combat skills. Which, me being me, makes Ulf distrust her even more. If Cheryl tells Ulf too much of the truth too soon, Gaia's visions say the plan to kill the Hivemother will fail.

When you set up any kind of conflict -- internal, external, or romantic -- it needs to make the characters' lives hell repeatedly throughout the book. If you notice your book's pacing slows, that's a good spot for one of these conflicts to create trouble. Make it painfully obvious that as bad as the external conflict is, the romantic and internal conflicts make it even worse.

Here's the first major romantic conflict clash in *Master of Honor*. Arthur has sent Ulf to find out what the hell is going on with his ex. One thing leads to another, and the two make love. But in the aftermath, everything goes sideways as Cheryl discovers once again that she can't trust the man she loves.

His eyes bored into hers, intense, earnest. So incredibly blue. "Whatever you think of me, believe this. Those eleven years with you were the best in my life. I've never been loved the way you loved me. I had never *felt* such love. I never will. The last thing I want to do is hurt you any more than I already have."

"Your timing always was impeccable," she muttered. She'd never felt so alone in her life. If Gaia was right about the alien scout, she might not survive the coming fight. If she was honest, that was the real reason she was so pissed off.

She craved Ulf's strength and protection with a ferocity that matched her body's helpless need for his.

He took another step closer and lowered his head. Cheryl found herself lifting her face. His mouth covered hers in a soft apology of a kiss. A plea for understanding. His arms slid around her until she felt surrounded by his strength. And despite her common sense, she felt almost... safe. *Ulf will protect me*, insisted the small, irrational voice that had always loved him. *This time, Ulf won't let me down.* (*Whenever a character thinks something like that early in the romance, it's time to shoot that tender moment in the head.*)

Gaia's voice rang in her mind. *Don't fight.* (*Gaia knows what's coming, and being a manipulative bitch, wants it to happen because it's necessary to her plants. Gaia, like Ulf, makes Cheryl's life hell. Create conflict in every relationship you possibly can.*)

"I'm sorry," Ulf whispered. "But there are lives at stake."

Her eyes widened, but before she could wrench

back, his arms clamped tight, pinning her as he lifted her off the floor. From the corner of one eye, she saw a wavering oval open in the air. Terror stabbed into her heart with a knife of ice. "Uuuulfff!"

They fell sideways through the dimensional gate.

* * *

As they hit the floor, Ulf twisted to take the impact on his back. The gate snapped closed, leaving them safely in the Mageverse. Light exploded in his face with a flare of hot pain that brought tears to his eyes. His grip loosened.

Cheryl catapulted off him. "You motherfucking son of a whore!" (*I don't ordinarily have one of my heroines curse her hero like that. Yet Cheryl needs to have a furious reaction to demonstrate how betrayed she feels. I also needed to motivate her reaction, which in turn makes Ulf distrust her.*)

"*Mom!*" Adam protested.

Ulf shook his head to clear it, then rolled to his feet despite the way the room spun. *She headbutted me.* He was astonished a mortal could hit that fast, that hard -- especially with her own forehead. Caught him dead in the nose, too, judging by the flood of salty copper dripping down his upper lip and into his mouth. "Cheryl, we just want to…"

He took a step forward -- and froze, staring up the length of one of his own swords into Cheryl's glaring eyes. Her lips were curled in a vicious snarl. The rapier's point was a fraction of an inch from his carotid, held in a white-knuckled grip.

He whipped a hand up, meaning to smash it against the flat of the blade and knock it aside so he could take the weapon from her. Instead, the blade flicked around his hand, avoiding the block to come to rest against his throat again. She'd done it every bit as fast and smoothly as one of the Knights. No mortal should have been that fast. Hell, most Majae couldn't have done it.

Ice rolled over him -- and it wasn't fear for himself. He knew Cheryl was still in there. He'd recognized the look in her eyes while they'd made love, the passion and keen intelligence he knew so well. (*Romantic conflict is vital in a romance, but both characters must have logical reasons to distrust each other. It can't be motivated by a stupid misunderstanding, and you can't just turn one of your protagonists into an asshole for no good reason.*)

But now she wasn't moving like the woman he loved at all. And he didn't recognize the murderous fury in her eyes. Yeah, she had reason to be pissed, but... *Did Gaia just take over? Is this a magical case of multiple personalities?* It was possible. When you were immortal, you eventually saw *everything* at least once. (*Ulf's in denial here. He doesn't want to admit Cheryl herself is that furious at him. Protagonists should be as prone to self-deception as anyone else. It makes them seem more human.*)

The point of the blade indented his skin as she glared into his eyes. "Really? You involved our *son* in this? He's not like you. He can't just betray the people he loves." (*Nobody can hurt you like someone you love, since they know you better than you do yourself. That's one of the things that makes a strong romantic conflict fascinating. It also cranks up the tension even higher than any murderous killer, since it hurts the lovers on an intimate level. Which is why Adam's Maja wife tries to intercede.*)

"Cheryl, this isn't necessary." Opal sounded utterly controlled. "Nobody wants to hurt you. But that's going to change if you use that sword on a Knight of the Round Table." (*This adds to the physical danger Cheryl is in. The situation is even more threatening because Gaia's magic doesn't work in the Mageverse. She's effectively powerless.*)

Managing to tear his gaze from those lethal hazel eyes, he studied the filigreed hilt in Cheryl's hand. It was one of a pair of dueling rapiers that hung on the library wall. How had she gotten it down so fast?

Her strength and speed are more than human. He'd suspected as much from the way she'd pulled him off the floor -- with one hand and him on his knees. And that from a sitting position on the couch, though he outweighed her by more than a hundred pounds.

It wasn't just the strength. Thanks to Gaia's magic, she now looked just as she had the day he'd met her. The same beautiful brunette hair, though longer now, curling around her shoulders. The same wide hazel eyes, delicate oval face and full, soft mouth. The lush, long-legged body. She'd been a witty, intelligent girl, charming as a songbird. A shaft of idealistic sunlight piercing his cynical night. (*Yes, the songbird thing is condescending as hell, and yes, that's on purpose. The man grew up in the Dark Ages. Sometimes it shows. He may be an immortal warrior, but he can be as big a dumbass as any other guy. You want that in your protagonist. As novelist Jim Butcher says, "Good books are about people making bad decisions.")*

But if the face was the same, the eyes were a different story. Where once there'd been a young woman's pure, uncomplicated love, now she watched him like an enemy. "So that whole seduction was a trap."

"No." He really hadn't planned it. "I just… got carried away." From the corner of one eye, he saw Adam's brows lift. Ulf winced as his cheeks began to heat.

"Calling bullshit on that one, 'Paul.' You don't *get* carried away on a job."

He needed to put an end to this. She was stronger than human, but he was still a vampire. And he had fifteen centuries of combat experience she lacked. Besides, she was bluffing. If *that's Cheryl. Well, there's one way to find out. (Ulf keeps underestimating Cheryl. Later in the book she accuses Arthur of seeing mortals the way people do housecats: we may love them, but we don't see them as equals. This is also true of Ulf. This scene illustrates the beginning of his character arc toward learning to respect Cheryl's ability and courage. But after having her act like a murderous wench, I need to show that she really does love Ulf, asshole or not.)*

He pressed into the sword's point, felt blood roll down his throat. Her angry eyes widened just a hair. The blade flicked down, pressed against the center of his chest.

"That's close enough."

"No." He stepped forward, hands spread wide. She retreated smoothly, refusing to let him impale himself.

But her gaze was narrow and steady. And she moved like one of the older warriors who'd been fighting for centuries. She wasn't even breathing hard, and there was a cold steadiness to the weapon that surprised him. To his knowledge, she'd never even touched a sword. That kind of skill took centuries to acquire. *That's got to be Gaia. She's taken over.*

The thought chilled him.

* * *

All romantic conflict comes down to trust. *Can I trust this person not to hurt me?* Ulf hurt Cheryl and lied to her because he had no choice. Telling her the truth would have triggered a catastrophe.

Now that Cheryl and Gaia are united in the plan to kill the aliens of the Hive, she can't tell Ulf about the threat because it would trigger a catastrophe. (It is, in fact, the same catastrophe. The Mageverse Seer saw that Ulf's being honest with Cheryl would lead to the destruction of humanity, though she didn't See why. If Ulf had told Cheryl the truth, she wouldn't have been the hostage when the Fomorians demanded his ring. Gaia wouldn't have been able to possess her, so they'd fail to prevent the Hive invasion.)

Whenever you have a coincidence like that -- two Seers seeing a vision of something -- you've got to make sure it's not a coincidence. It must all be related. In this case, Merlin, the Maja Seer, and Gaia all have the same vision: the extinction of humanity. That makes sense. Anything that nasty would show up in a lot of visions.

Throughout the rest of the book, Ulf finds himself having to choose whether to trust Cheryl. She gradually wins him over. It helps that the Magekind themselves piss him off by mistreating her.

Next, we'll examine the climactic fight where Ulf and Cheryl must confront their demons and trust each other. I'll also explain why I made the choices I did in the fight itself.

Chapter Six: Love is a Battlefield

Climax Construction

Whenever I go into a climax, I try to engineer a situation that forces the characters to resolve their internal and romantic conflicts to defeat the villain. If you aren't writing a romance, you should use the protagonist's internal conflict and its wound to add an additional level of difficulty.

Cheryl's internal conflict is that though she was an ordinary woman a few months ago, now she's got to prevent the extinction of humanity. Her romantic conflict is that Ulf has betrayed her too many times and she doesn't trust him. Thus, the climax must force her to trust both herself *and* Ulf.

Ulf's conflicts are born of the fact that he doesn't have a high opinion of mortal abilities -- especially those of mortal women. For them to win this fight, he must trust Cheryl to survive her battle with the Hive. He must also follow her plan and ignore his instinct to protect her.

From a storytelling standpoint, I had another consideration. My Mageverse vampires and witches have been fighting all kinds of critters since 2004. One of the key sources of dopamine is surprise, so I needed to find a way to surprise my longtime readers.

That's one reason why I made Gaia's magic completely different from the Magekind's. Instead of being will-based, as theirs is, hers acts more like electricity -- it requires a crystal network to focus its power, as wiring carries electricity. This is another thing that freaks the Magekind out -- why does this woman have all this crystal winding through her body?

I had to force Ulf to let Cheryl fight by herself to

prove he's changed. That catches him in a massive internal conflict he must resolve.

Also, I've shown Knights of the Round Table and Ulf in particular fight before, so it wouldn't be new to my readers. I could have had him and Cheryl fight as a team, but he'd have taken over. I wanted the focus on my heroine, just as in *Arcane Betrayal*, I let Grant Sawyer, my plain vanilla hero, take the lead in that climax. I had to keep my heroine, Margay Whitfield -- and her magical tiger spirit -- out of the action until later in the fight.

Trust Issues

Heading into the climax, Gaia finally permits Cheryl to tell Ulf that the two of them must defeat the Hive without involving the rest of the Magekind. If Arthur interferes, Gaia's visions predict the Hive will win. They must lure Hivemother, the Hive's queen, into showing up personally to feed on Cheryl's power and life force. Ulf *can't* tell Arthur the truth. He must disobey the man he's been loyal to for fifteen centuries.

For once, he has to choose Cheryl.

Ulf's role in the fight is to use the Destroyer, an enchanted spear Merlin created that can kill the Hivemother -- and with her, the Hive. But if Ulf uses the weapon on the scout before Hivemother arrives, she'll be scared off, and they'll lose the opportunity to kill her. Hivemother and the Hive will attack in force and destroy all life on Earth.

The couple get their chance when they learn the Hive scout has set a trap for Cheryl at the hospital where she works as a nurse. As Ulf watches, hidden behind an invisibility spell with the Destroyer, Cheryl fights the shape-shifting scout.

* * *

When the magic vanished, the thing no longer looked remotely human. It was vaguely insectoid, with four stick legs and two arms. A thick tail whipped around its body, tipped with a vicious spike like a scorpion's. Segmented plates covered its body, and three close-set compound eyes glared from a round head equipped with jutting mandibles. It was as black as an oil spill, complete with iridescent sheen. (*When you begin a fight, you need to establish what the antagonist looks like and what weapons they have.*)

Clawed feet clicked on the laminated wood flooring. The click became a clatter as it charged Cheryl in a blur.

Ulf, invisible, raised his pike... and swore, remembering the plan. He stepped aside to let the thing skitter past.

Cheryl whirled and ran, stiff-arming the automated doors. They slammed open as she sprinted through. Mandibles clicking, the creature clattered after her. Ulf bit back a curse and ran after it. He knew she hadn't panicked. Not Cheryl. She was luring it away from all the sick, unconscious mortals. (*He's finally learned to respect Cheryl's courage. Trouble is, he loves her. It goes against every instinct he has to do nothing as she fights for her life. All she has in the way of weaponry are claws and Gaia's alien armor, which appears formed of metallic feathers. Her apparent lack of defenses is all part of the trap for Hivemother.*)

The bug was gaining. The thing's spiked tail lashed, and it gathered itself to leap. Ulf's heart pounded as his hands tightened on the pike. The hall doglegged in front of her, but Cheryl leaped, hit the wall with one foot, and kicked herself backward into a somersault. She landed astride the creature, her weight smashing it to the floor.

Ulf blinked. *Damn. Gaia* has *been training her.* (*Normally, I'd use my fighting protagonist as the viewpoint character. But in this case, I'm in Ulf's POV to let you see his internal conflict. He* must *prove he's learned something over the course of the book. Too, the question of whether he can resist the urge to interfere adds to the tension.*)

The bug's spiked tail lashed up and slammed into her shoulder, rebounding off the feathered armor. Cheryl ignored the impact, driving those long spiked claws into the armored plates that protected the thing's neck.

The tail punched again, once, twice, drops of black venom flying. She kept right on digging at the armor, grim and determined. (*Now I need the bad guy to do something different, since what it's doing now isn't working. You have to put yourself in your villain's shoes -- or in this case, claws.*)

The tail whipped around her torso, jerked her off the creature, and smashed her backward into the wall. He heard her gasp of pain and felt his every muscle tense with the need to do save her. (*The protagonists must suffer in a fight, so the reader feels they've earned their victory. The harder the characters battle, the bigger the dopamine payoff for the reader when they win. The more you hurt your character, the more the reader will enjoy their cathartic victory.*)

As Ulf watched, unable to do a damned thing, the

bug thing reared onto its back legs and lunged at Cheryl's throat, mandibles spread wide. (*When you're writing a fight, visualize where the characters' bodies and limbs are, and how each can attack or defend themselves. What would* you *do? Is there a way you can surprise the reader with the unexpected?*)

She slammed an arm up, ramming her forearm into the mandibles as she punched the claws of her free hand into its eyes. (*Note the action verbs I use: slammed, ramming, punched. All three of those could have been replaced with "hit," but they all communicate different degrees of force and create different mental images. I want Cheryl to fight with the kind of brutality you need in a desperate fight to the death. Having her dig her claws into the creature's eyes illustrates the point.*)

The thing screeched in agony and tried to rear away, but Cheryl whipped both legs around its torso. Wrapping clawed hands around its head, she shoved violently backward. Chitinous plates creaked as she fought to break it in half. (*Breaking someone in half isn't an act we associate with women. Having her do this illustrates both her strength and ruthlessness.*)

The creature skittered backward, trying to tear free as it raked at her with clawed arms.

"This might have worked for you last time," Cheryl snarled, "but I've made upgrades since then." Opening her mouth, she breathed a boiling cloud of magic into the creature's face. (*Now, whenever you trot out an ability like that in a fight, you should foreshadow it so the reader won't think you wrote yourself into a corner and cheated to get out of it.*

Though Cheryl hasn't breathed magic like this earlier in the book, we've seen Gaia use that power before.)

Its head burst into black flame. Burning, it made a sound so high-pitched, Ulf thought his ears would bleed as it lashed and writhed in Cheryl's merciless grip.

Something cracked, and the thing broke in half, collapsing beneath her, upper half ablaze.

Ulf blinked, a little stunned at the violence of the fight and her vicious efficiency. *What the hell did she need me for? And what about the plan?* (*That thought is a question the reader would logically be asking. Having Ulf ask it shows it isn't a plot hole.*)

Cheryl leaped up and scrambled away as the flames died. Crouching, she fixed her eyes on the dead bug like a cat watching a rathole. Sure enough, magic boiled up around the thing, spinning and expanding.

Uh-oh. The cloud expanded as Cheryl danced backward. The magic abruptly sucked inward. Where the dead creature had been, a massive *thing* loomed, almost brushing the ceiling. It looked like a cross between a troll and Godzilla, complete with violet scales that covered its massive frame, a dinosaur-like head, and huge clawed hands. It had to weigh well over five hundred pounds. (*Make matters worse for your protagonist during the climax. Every time the reader thinks your characters have the antagonist on the ropes, the villain needs to counter with something even more deadly. Keep the reader thinking, "Oh, crap! How are they going to get out of this?"*)

A chill rolled over Ulf. Was this a different warrior, or had the first one come back from the dead? Either way, he wouldn't have wanted to fight it, and he was a fucking vampire. His heart sank. *Merlin's Cup, she's got no prayer.* (*Your protagonist's fear for their lover intensifies the reader's tension. You want your characters to have confidence in their abilities, but they must be acutely aware they can lose -- and the deadly stakes if they do.*)

It hissed, red eyes glittering above its mouthful of fangs, and charged. She watched it come. Ulf readied the pike, moving forward, eyes locking on the joint between the lizard's skull and its thick neck.

But the instant before the lizard could strike, Cheryl sidestepped with a graceful twist of her shoulders. Godzilla's fist missed her by inches and rammed into the lobby wall. It fractured like an eggshell with an explosive crunch, filling the air with dust and flying concrete chips.

The creature's fist was sunk in the hole all the way to one scaly elbow. It jerked back, but it was trapped.

Cheryl darted in, ducking under its extended body. Claws flashed as she raked Godzilla's ribs. The attack didn't do a damn thing as it finally jerked free and lunged at her head. Fanged jaws snapped a hair's breadth from her face as she arched away, back-fisting the creature across the muzzle. (*If the thing is trying to bite her face, she'd have to arch backward to avoid it. She needs to counter-attack. She's in position for a punch, but a backhand always seems to have an element of surprise and contempt to it.*)

It roared and swung dagger length claws, raking her shoulder as she leaped clear.

Hissing, it went after her with both clawed hands in a vicious series of raking attacks. She ducked, twisted, and leaped, somehow avoiding every blow with lithe agility, her own claws slashing at any part of the thing she could reach. But no matter how many times she hit it, her claws glanced off its scales. (*Since every critter needs to be more deadly than the one before, making it invulnerable to her claws ups the tension.*)

Until, with a frustrated curse, she raced around behind the thing and scampered up its back like an organ grinder's monkey. She whipped something long, thin and glowing around Godzilla's neck, snapped her legs around the lizard's massive torso and hauled backward with all her strength, twisting the cord tight.

A magical garrote. Must've conjured it. (*As I've said, every fight must end in something spectacular and unexpected. Having her scramble up this monster's back is nuts, and so is her garroting it.*)

The muscles in her narrow back rolled under her feathered armor with the violence of her pull. Godzilla reeled backward, gagging and hissing, caught itself, jacked forward to catch its balance, then slammed backward down onto its back, landing directly on top of her. Cheryl cried out its weight crashed down on her. (*If she's on top of it, a creature that big is naturally going to try to crush her.*)

Shit!

Ulf advanced, readying the pike to thrust. Smoke sizzled from the scaled flesh beneath the cord. Which made this the perfect opening. Eying the lizard's gasping jaws, he saw he could ram the pike up through its palate and into its brain...

Then he noticed Cheryl was furiously shaking her head, though she didn't say a word. A signal meant for him -- Not yet.

Centuries of combat experience howled in revolt. If you ignored an opening this good, you could end up regretting it. (*As a knight of the Round Table, Ulf has been in a hell of a lot of fights over fifteen centuries. I figured a big part of his conflict was the same experience and training that made him an elite warrior.*)

But Cheryl knew what she was doing. She'd fought this thing before -- or at least Gaia had. He needed to have a long talk with her about working with partners if they both survived this mess.

Godzilla's massive fist slammed into one arm, but she hung on, hauling back until the garrote indented the scaled throat. Harder, until the creature arched halfway off the floor, tearing at her arms with its claws. Alien blood flowed around the glowing cord as it bit deeper. Deeper. Until it abruptly blazed white-hot and jerked all the way through the thing's neck. (*Not that I emphasize how long and hard she has to pull while it claws her. It can never be easy.*)

The head popped off Godzilla's shoulders and tumbled across the floor, trailing blood as it rolled. The massive neck stump pumped, splashing the wall a deep cobalt blue.

Before Ulf could bend to haul it off her, she grabbed its shoulders and shoved, rolling the massive corpse off herself. She fell back, gasping for air.

How strong *was* she, anyway?

Ulf started to speak, but she was shaking her head again, one hand lifted in warning even as she rolled to her feet and scrambled clear.

Oh shit. It's going to come to life again. (*You always want to end a scene break during a fight on a cliffhanger.*)

* * *

Are you sure the Errul doesn't have the Destroyer? Hivemother hissed in Valac's mind. He suppressed his irritation and alarm at the question, lest she detect it. Hivemother could invade his brain -- even take possession of his physical being -- any time she cared to. Every member of the Hive was, after all, ultimately an extension of her consciousness. (*When I'm writing flunkies like Valac, I love to show that the henchmen have their own agendas that may be in opposition to the Big Bad's. This can introduce an element of unpredictability as the reader wonders if the flunky will betray their boss. By the way, Errul is the name of Gaia's people.*)

I feel no trace of it, he told her as he recalled his magic, dissolving the combat form the Errul had killed. *If the Errul had it, she would surely have ended me by now.*

He groped through the memory of the Hive's

many victims for a template of a more suitable form. He needed one with the power to defeat the Errul. She might not possess the Destroyer at present, but power still blazed around her like a star. The conduit between her and her home universe pulsed with magic, tempting and menacing at once. (*One thing I hadn't done is explain how the scout can assume all these shapes. I reasoned that if the Hive fed on life force, it could call on the shapes of its victims. And the Hive have killed some seriously nasty creatures.*)

Indeed, Hivemother said. *What a feast she will be. Take her for me, Valac, and the next two matings will be yours.*

In the deepest level of his mind, where even Hivemother couldn't hear, he thought, *Assuming I live to claim it*. She hadn't felt the force of the Errul's blows. How anyone using a human form could attack with such speed and power, he had no idea. They were such fragile, powerless creatures.

Vengeance definitely was not. (*Vengeance is the name the Hive gave Gaia. It's a good idea to show scenes from the antagonist's point of view, because it makes them more believable. Too, giving a villain goals and internal conflicts make them more three-dimensional. When you're writing something as weird as the Hive, every little bit helps.*)

Strike her down, Hivemother purred, eager greed in her psychic voice. *Strike her down and let me take her!*

* * *

Now I'm finally going into Cheryl's POV to show how frightened she really is. If the protagonist isn't afraid, the reader isn't going to worry. And that worry will make the protagonist's eventual victory sweeter for the reader.

You'll notice Cheryl easily won the first couple of fights with the Hive scout. I wouldn't ordinarily do that in a climax, but here I'm setting the reader up for a reversal.

Grimly, Cheryl watched the black roiling magic as the scout began to reform again. She ached everywhere, and she suspected one of her ribs was broken despite her armor. She'd thought that purple lizard was going to smash her like a cockroach. It had certainly hit her hard enough.

But Cheryl had survived, mostly because of the raw power blazing through her. Gaia was pumping so much magic into her crystal-augmented bones and muscles, it felt like drinking from a fire hose.

It was also more than a little terrifying, because it illustrated just how bad the spirit thought this fight was going to be. (*Juicing the tension a little. Making the reader wait to see what kind of creature she'll be facing next adds to that.*)

Pacing grimly, Cheryl watched the black cloud suck inward, revealing her newest opponent. She recoiled. *The fuck is that?*

I have no idea, Gaia said. *Something from another universe.*

It was even bigger than the lizard, towering two

feet taller than Cheryl, with four massive arms and two legs supporting a huge, misshapen body as pallid as a slug. A ring of eyes encircled its bulbous head, and it had no nose, only a series of slits running along its barrel chest. She suspected they were gills, judging by the way they opened and closed. *Looks like a good place to sink my claws.*

Assuming she dared get that close. Something she was in no hurry to do, because the thing's mouth took up most of its head. The lipless circle was lined with serrated teeth, all pointed inward. It reminded her of the thing that tried to eat Luke Skywalker in *Return of the Jedi*.

Shit. Anything that goes into that mouth, I won't get back. (With creatures like this, an element of horror helps worry the reader even more as they wonder what this thing is capable of.)

It advanced toward her, dropping down on the knuckles of its lower set of hands to walk like a gorilla. The upper set of hands flexed, claws flashing as muscle rolling along massive arms.

All those crimson eyes glared at her as it opened its jaws wide. Which gave her a great view down its throat, lined with yet more inward pointing teeth.

Holy shit! It's teeth all away down. Cheryl had never wanted to run screaming like a little girl so badly in her entire life. And never with such excellent cause.

If you do, Gaia told her in an icy voice, *that thing will kill everyone in this hospital, including Brandon and every baby in the NICU.*

Cheryl's mind instantly flashed the horrific image of one of those massive hands picking up a preemie and... (*More stakes, as if she doesn't have enough. But what the character values reveals who they are. In Cheryl's case, she's more worried about the babies than herself.*)

Don't think! Gaia snapped. *Move!*

Cheryl dragged magic from Gaia's conduit, conjuring a pair of *wakizashi*. The short Japanese swords filled her hands, sparks dancing along the steel. There wasn't enough room to swing a longer sword. With a howl of terror and fury, she sprang at the thing.

One of those enormous hands snapped toward her face. *No way to dodge -- it's going to tear my head off...*

A wave of magic wrapped around her, flipping her toward the ceiling. Gaia, finally doing something. The huge fist missed her by half an inch. *You do the attacking*, Gaia snapped. *I'll navigate.* (*Gaia has held off throughout the fight to let Cheryl learn how to handle herself in a vicious battle. The fact she wades in now reveals how serious the situation is, juicing the tension again.*)

Another magical burst sent her shooting toward the scout's massive skull like a rebounding cue ball. With a shrieking cry, the creature jerked aside so fast, Cheryl barely saw it at all. She managed to slash the blade across thick, pallid hide even as she flew by. (*You want your protagonist to attack every time they get the chance. She's flying past, so she's going to cut Big, Bad and Ugly.*)

Sparks snapped, filling the air with ozone and the smell of burning meat. The scout screeched like nails over a blackboard. (*Sensory details add to the reality of the scene. Pick unpleasant ones -- burning meat, nails on a blackboard. Though in retrospect, I should have edited that last one -- too cliché.*)

She bounced off the nearest wall, twisting in midair in a way that should have been impossible for any human with a spine. A massive white hand missed her face as Gaia propelled her past, and she cut with both blades, ripping them across the creature's arm in an X shaped cut. She hit the ground behind it, spun and leaped, slamming into the thing's back, knees bending to absorb the impact. Pain exploded in her left upper thigh as she landed badly on her twisting target. She ignored it, cutting across the massive neck, then dove backward toward the floor. (*You want your character to feel pain and fear yet keep fighting anyway. When the character does something dangerous, like jumping on top of an opponent, have them get hurt doing it. It will add to the realism of the scene. This adds to the character's heroism if they keep fighting anyway.*)

This time she didn't see the hand coming. One of the lower set grabbed her by an ankle and slung her at the nearest wall. (*When you've got a monster opponent, let him remind the reader how nasty he really is. In a fight, you grab whatever comes to hand. Grabbing her by the arm wouldn't have created the same sense of chaos.*)

Her back whipsawed so hard, she thought it would break.

I didn't reinforce your spine for nothing.

The wall shot toward her face. Instead of splattering her brain all over it, she hit what felt like an invisible mattress and rebounded.

Gaia's magic.

She hit the ground, turning the fall into a tumbling roll, somehow holding onto her swords. As she sprawled on her back, her ankle blazed with pain and the side of her face felt numb. She had no idea what had hit her head. One eye was beginning to swell. Before she could somersault upright, massive feet crashed down on either side of her body as fists the size of her torso blurred toward her face. (*Here comes that coup de grâce -- the spectacular ending move of the fight.*)

She curled into a ball and threw up a magical shield an instant before the thing's punches hit. Roaring in fury, the monster bent over her, slamming blow after blow into her shield. With every impact, sparks exploded from the shield as Cheryl huddled under it. Feeding more magic into the barrier, she clutched her swords and watched for an opening.

The pummeling was so savage, she could feel the floor cracking under her as the force rolled through her shield.

We're on the tenth floor. If it gives way, we'll kill whoever's below us. Hell, the entire hospital could collapse, considering how much power that fucker's throwing off. And since I put everybody to sleep, they can't evacuate. I've got to stop the bastard before he kills us all! (*Adding some stakes. Again, whenever you can make things worse for the protagonist, do.*)

She watched through her raised arms, timing the blows. In the heartbeat after one fist rebounded, and before the descent of the other, she reached into the conduit, dragged in all the magic she could, and dropped her shield, meaning to blast the creature in the face...

Something hit her head from both sides so hard, she saw nothing but an explosion of light.

He has four arms, Gaia reminded her. (*If you're fighting a creature with four arms, you might lose track of that in the heat of the action -- especially if it's beating the hell out of you at the time. This makes getting hit with the extra set the perfect ending blow.*)

Above her, the creature's huge mouth opened.

Shield! Shield, damn it! But her dazed brain could only fumble for the power. *Gaia!*

Too late. The scout breathed a magical blast that rolled over her in a searing wave of agony. She couldn't even manage a scream.

Everything fell away into blackness. (*That's this story's literal black moment when all seems lost. Every climactic battle needs a moment when both the characters and the reader think the protagonists are dead.*)

* * *

There! Hivemother shrieked in triumph. *She is ours!*

But Valac had remembered the last fight with the Errul. *I don't think...*

But Hivemother had already rolled through the psychic bond between them, hunger driving her to recklessness.

Who could blame her? In that heartbeat, as the prey lay unconscious, all the Errul's great magic undefended, her conduit to her universe's power still open wide.

And it had been too long since the Hivemother had fed. She seized Valac's mind and body, ready to drink down the Errul's luscious power…

* * *

Consciousness returned, accompanied by agonizing pain.

Cheryl's brain seemed to burn, as if her neurons were made of lava. She screamed in the prison of her body -- and made no sound.

I have you, Gaia said. *I will protect you.*

Against what? For a moment Cheryl had no idea why everything hurt. What the hell was going on?

Her eyes blinked open… and she thought she was having a nightmare. The thing that hovered over her face was white, lumpy and misshapen. The ring of eyes that encircled the round head were compound, like those of a fly. And its gaping mouth revealed row after row teeth gleaming down into the darkness of its throat. She tried to scream. (*Let the reader share the character's terror by describing every ugly detail.*)

Remember the plan!

Oh, fuck, if this doesn't work… She stared up into the

serrated teeth and prayed as she hadn't prayed since Ulf had walked out.

* * *

Ulf stared in horror, every instinct he had at war. The creature had pinned Cheryl to the floor under its massive weight. She looked like a two-year-old beneath it.

Use the pike! The hell with Gaia's plan -- it isn't working! She was nowhere near that thing's weight class, no matter what Gaia had done to her. *I can't just stand here and watch it* eat *her!*

Which was when the surface of the massive creature began to ripple, as if someone had thrown pebbles into a lake. The ripples spread, strengthened into waves, shooting fissures through the thing as if it were breaking apart.

What the hell is happening?

The creature exploded into countless black flakes that rained down over Cheryl, covering her like an onyx snowfall.

Jesu, what now? He froze, staring down at the mound of spiked black crystals that blanketed her. They resembled giant obsidian snowflakes that turned and writhed in slow waves, as if alive and breathing. Like some alien colony creature.

Which, if Gaia was right, was exactly what they were.

He drew back the pike, preparing to thrust it downward. Hesitated. His hands trembled, making the tip of the weapon shake. *What if I'm jumping the gun*?

And then, as if from a great distance away, he heard Cheryl's voice, strangled, emerging from the mound of colony cells. Sounding as if the flakes filled her mouth. Choked her. *"Now,* Ulf!"

With a gasp of relief, he thrust the lance into the mass. And hoped to God he didn't hit Cheryl.

The moment the pike made contact, a wave of alien magic shot from the head's spear point, pulsing across the colony in leaping blue sparks. The flakes stiffened for a moment, glittering in the magical light.

A second pulse flowed across the mass and flashed up the shaft of the lance, blazing and crackling. A counterattack! Pain seared his hands as the alien magic lashed him. Agony seared his jerking muscles, and he almost lost his grip on the lance.

No, damn it! He was the only hope she had. He clung to the lance in stubborn rage, fighting not to thrust too deep and hit Cheryl. (*You need to imagine the practical implications of attacks. If you're stabbing a spear into a pile of black aliens with your wife beneath it, you'd naturally worry that you'd hit her. I also needed to make the attack as painful for Ulf as for Cheryl -- he must show the reader that he deserves his seat on the Round Table.*)

Wave after wave of alien magic blasted him, dancing over his armor in vicious crackling pops. If it hadn't been for the suit, it would have fried him like a mosquito in a bug zapper.

He'd failed Cheryl twenty-eight years ago. He damn well wasn't going to fail her now. Teeth gritted, he clung to the haft, smelling his palms begin to burn even through his gauntlets as sparks tore up and down the weapon.

This time, Cheryl, I'm not going anywhere! (*Ulf finally shows he can be trusted -- and so can Cheryl.*)

* * *

Cheryl heard Gaia screaming. Not with her ears, but with her very bones, her muscles, her skin, until her entire body vibrated like an amplifier. The spirit seized the spell in the lance and drove it into the heart of the Hive, forcing it into Hivemother with every bit of power she'd hoarded over the past fifteen hundred years.

Gaia had failed her people all those centuries ago, and they'd died. Nor had they been the only ones. Every planet where the Hive had committed genocide since had paid the price for Gaia's failure. *It ends here.*

Cheryl could feel the furious energies of the conduit thundering around her like Niagara Falls, channeling the death spell from the pike. And yet she herself was protected in the tight cocoon of magic Gaia had spun around her. The spirit's last gift, Cheryl's reward for agreeing to become both weapon -- and bait. (*The reasons for Gaia's actions haven't been clear to either Cheryl or the reader. I need to clarify all that in the end of the fight, but I have to do it quickly. That means keeping the explanation as short and clear as possible. To do that, you must be prepared to edit the hell out of the explanation as many times as it takes. Editing is the difference between good writing and mediocre story-telling.*)

Gaia had known the Hivemother would not be able to resist all that seductive power in such an apparently vulnerable package. Now Gaia could finally do what her people had created her for -- feeding all the conduit's thundering magic into the spell she'd stored in the lance.

The Hivemother's dying shrieks seemed to stab into Cheryl's skull like an ice pick. The rest of the Hive screeched in echo as the spell ripped them all apart, as it should have done fifteen centuries ago -- avenging Gaia's people and all the others who'd fed the Hive since.

And as they died, it seemed to Cheryl she heard a great, psychic roar she somehow recognized.

The ghosts of the Errul.

There were others too. She felt their names vibrating in that cry -- the Ji and ki'c, the People of the Sun, the Gibwr, the CoeoItchir and the Utilivis. All the inhabitants of murdered worlds without number. The triumphant chorus of the avenged built, drowning out even the Hive's screams.

Then, as if cut with a knife, the song of Vengeance stopped.

Silence. (*I wanted to show that Gaia and Humanity aren't the only ones the Hive has targeted. They've been committing genocide for millennia, and I liked the idea of their victims' ghosts shouting in triumph.*)

Cheryl's skull seemed to throb with the psychic echoes of the Vengeance. But there was no more sense of the Hive's endless, vicious hunger.

Hardly daring to hope, Cheryl breathed, *Gaia?*

Yes?

It was the spirit's voice, but it sounded so faint. Barely audible instead of its usual psychic thunder. *Are you all right?*

I have never been better. They are gone.

Completely? It worked?

Oh yes. You were magnificent. So brave.

You don't... you don't sound right. Fear pierced Cheryl, fear she'd never expected to feel for the spirit who'd invaded her life. *Are you hurt?*

Dear girl, I'm dying. I had to feed all my power to the spell. Exterminating an entire race of psychic parasites takes a great deal of magic. I held back only enough to protect you.

Oh no! Cheryl opened the conduit, drew on it as Gaia had taught her to do. To her relief, the magic leapt to her will. She'd feared she'd lost access to it, considering how feeble Gaia sounded. Now all she had to do was feed that magic to the spirit. Recharge her.

Cheryl, I'm not an iPhone. My task is finished. My battle is won. I can rest. (Sometimes humor – "I'm not an iPhone" -- can break the tension in the wrong way. But I thought this line also showed Gaia's personality. Given that she's often seemed cold and distant, this makes her and her death seem real to the reader.)

No! Don't let go. I can save you, you don't have to

die... Cheryl began to pour magic into the spirit, driven by her nurse's instinct to heal.

It didn't work. Gaia simply... rejected the magic. *You need that power, child. You're your people's guardian now, as I once was mine,* Gaia whispered, faint as the distant rustle of dead leaves. *Thank you for helping me avenge my dead. Because of you, I do not die a failure.*

And then she was gone, melting away into the dark. (*The protagonists must pay a price for their victory. Sometimes it's the death of a character the reader cares about.*)

Ulf stared down at Cheryl in warring dread and hope. She lay in a halo of ash.

It had happened in a heartbeat. One minute he'd been fighting lashing waves of magic. The next, the obsidian flakes had blazed white and burned away. "Cheryl? Cheryl, baby, are you all right?" He tossed the lance aside and dropped to his knees as it clattered across the floor.

Hesitating, he eyed her. She could have injuries that didn't show through her feathered armor, so he repressed his instinct to haul her into his lap. Grinding his teeth, he muttered, "There's never a witch around when you need one. When you don't, they're all over you."

Carefully, he reached out to cup her cheek. At the contact, something popped, and the world around him went crystal clear. The invisibility spell had broken. But Cheryl still lay limp in her feathered armor. Which at least meant she was still alive -- the armor would have disappeared otherwise.

"Cheryl?" He stroked the slick, cool feathers over her cheek with his thumb. They felt so delicate, considering the raw power of the attacks they'd absorbed. "Cheryl, please -- open those beautiful eyes..."

Abruptly, she sucked in a whooping gust of air and began to cough. As he watched, the feathers vanished from her face, sinking into her body, leaving pale skin and nurse's scrubs behind.

He felt the same happening to his own, leaving him in the same T-shirt and jeans he'd been wearing at the start. "Come on, honey, you're scaring the hell out of me."

Her eyes flashed open, and she stared up at him, blinking, disoriented. Sudden tears spilled down her cheeks. "Ulf!" Jacking into a sitting position, she threw her arms around him with a strangled cry.

He gasped in relief and crushed her to him. "Thank Jesu! I thought you were dead!"

"Yeah, I thought that too, about six dozen times." She made a little sobbing sound. "Gaia *is* dead."

His eyes widened. *Oh, hell, is Cheryl mortal again?* And a savage heartbeat later -- *I don't give a damn if she is. I'm never walking away from her again. Arthur can go fuck himself.* He lowered his head and kissed her hard. Desperately.

She kissed him back. (*And there you get the flood of the dopamine wash. But there's one more antagonist they* must *confront to show they've changed.*)

"What the hell is going on here?"

The familiar bark made Ulf leap to his feet in sheer reflex, dragging Cheryl up and shoving her behind him.

Surrounded by the other Knights of the Round Table -- including Kel, along with Guinevere, Eva, Morgana, and Smoke -- Arthur glared at them. They all wore expressions of anger, bemusement or some combination of the two.

Arthur was simply pissed. His deep black eyes snapped in rage, teeth visibly grinding. "Kel went to check on you. Imagine his surprise when he found you gone. You want to tell me what the hell you're doing on Earth? In a hospital? *With someone who might be killing people!*"

Ulf wasn't in the mood for this shit. "I was watching my woman almost die trying to do *your* job -- save humanity. Which, thank you very much, she *succeeded in doing*."

Smoke, sitting on Eva's shoulder in house cat form, sniffed delicately. "Does smell like somebody threw a hell of a lot of power around. Among other things." He glanced at the massive hole the scout had punched in the back wall. "What did *that*?"

"Also," Morgana said, her gaze distant, "it seems every human in this building is unconscious."

"Gaia wanted to keep them out of the line of fire," Cheryl said. "It was safer to put them out."

Arthur turned the glare on her. "Hope none of

them was in surgery at the time." (*This is a question I needed to answer, and Arthur was the logical person to ask it.*)

"No, they hadn't started the next procedures yet, and the others were in recovery. Gaia checked. I'll wake them all in a minute."

"Why did you knock them out to begin with?" Suspicion narrowed Arthur's black eyes. (*Repetition on the black eyes there. I didn't catch that in the rewrite.*)

Ulf really didn't like his liege's body language. His right hand longed for the sword he'd left back in the Mageverse. Instead he stepped forward, planted his palm in the middle of Arthur's chest and pushed him back a step. Hard.

And had the pleasure of seeing black eyes widen in astonishment. Ulf wasn't on the list of people who got up in Arthur's face -- about *anything*.

"You forget yourself," Arthur snapped.

"No, you do. She damn near died saving us all. You're not going to bully her." (*To prove he really has changed, Ulf needs to stand up to Arthur, his sworn liege or not. When he tells Arthur that from now on, his first concern will be his wife, he means it. Any time you have a character giving your protagonist hell, you must have the protagonist confront them at some point. You don't want them to come off like a doormat. Later in the scene, Cheryl tells Arthur off. I needed both of them to demonstrate they weren't going to be pushed around anymore, not even by the Once and Future King.*)

Chapter Seven: Physical Chess

Fights have a simple logic that allows you to put them together like a chess game. Let's say we have two combatants, A and B.

First, the basic rule of a fight is that if A tries to hit B -- whether with a fist, a sword, or a bullet -- there are only two possibilities: the attack lands or it misses. Since the result can be serious injuries or even death, B must make sure the attack doesn't land.

To force A to miss, B has only three choices: block the blow, take cover, or dodge. Then B must counterattack before A can launch another attack.

At that point, A has the same choice: block, take cover, or dodge B's attack.

That's really all there is to it. You construct a fight one move at a time using that simple logic. Unfortunately, this can get monotonous if you're not careful. You must vary the choreography to keep things interesting. That's true in real life fights too. Predictability gives your opponent a chance to anticipate what you're going to do and take you out.

You should vary the weapons your characters use as well, creating surprise wherever you can. (**Surprise = Dopamine.**) A swordsman may punch his opponent to set him up for a lunge, or somebody might pick up a rock during a fistfight.

That's why a big fight requires a *lot* of planning. In fact, it may be the most complicated scene you write, especially if a large cast is involved. Either way, aim for maximum drama and surprise.

The key to making a fight dramatic lies more in the emotion and sensations the characters feel rather than the individual blows. Try to put yourself in the fight, imagining the pain, exhaustion, and fear of your characters.

Remember to use all five senses. What are they going to see, smell, taste, touch and hear? About any fight scene in any period -- past, present or future -- will include the reek of fear, sweat, and blood.

In a medieval, you'd also smell the metallic tang of armor, the musk of sweating horses, horse manure, leather, and smoke. You'd hear the creak of tack, the screams of wounded men, the buzz of circling flies. Men and women howling in fear or rage.

In a modern story, you might smell gasoline and gunpowder from fired ammo. In a futuristic, you'd smell ozone and exotic plastics.

You want to paint a verbal picture of the scene that is so vivid the reader can see it. However, too much description can slow the scene down. Use short, sharp sentences, and don't hesitate to throw in sentence fragments. Those effects will speed up your pacing and capture a sense of urgency and desperation.

Think about how these particular people would fight. Well-trained Navy SEALs are not going to fight like rednecks in a bar.

Here's a sample from *Warrior* (2008), the first book in my *Time Hunters* series. The heroine is an ordinary woman snatched out of a deep sleep by a cyborg killer. In this scene, I wanted to capture Jessica's sense of terror and confusion while establishing her courageous nature.

"Get up!" A huge hand locked in Jess's hair and jerked her off her bed, white-hot agony flaring through her scalp. Jarred violently awake, she yelped and grabbed at the fist tangled in her long mane. Through tears of shock and confusion, she saw a man looming over her, the silhouette of immense shoulders blocking the dim light from the window. Teeth flashed in a snarl. "Where is she? Where's the heretic?" (*The word "Heretic" is designed to show the reader that this guy is more than the stereotypical serial killer. That would be terrifying enough, but if you don't know what drives this guy, that makes it even worse.*)

He flung her against the wall so hard, she felt the Sheetrock crack. Stars exploded behind her eyes as her head snapped back against the wall. "What?" Jess yelled. "Who the hell are --" (*Remember that a hard blow often has two impacts: the blow itself and hitting the nearest hard surface. Think of the physics of the blow.*)

"Shut up!" Hot breath flooded against her skin as a face shoved inches from her own. Something cold pricked her throat as a massive body pinned her. Whatever he was wearing felt oddly slick and scaly, more like snakeskin than fabric. "Where is she?" (*Note the five senses: the Sheetrock cracking, stars exploding in her head, his hot breath, the cold point of his knife, the scaled sensation of his suit.*)

"Who?" She swung at him with all the ferocity her trailer park childhood had taught her. (*Though an ordinary human, Jess has courage. Try to show the heroic core of your protagonist, because that will build reader sympathy.*)

Light flared behind her eyes again. She tasted blood, heard a metallic ringing. He'd punched her. (*He hits her so fast she doesn't even see the blow coming. I wanted to try to depict how it would feel being in the grip of a guy like that when he starts beating you -- how disorienting and terrifying it would be.*)

"Your roommate! Where did she go?"

Like she'd tell him a damn thing. "Get off me!"

The sting of cold pain intensified against her throat. "Do you want to die?" He bared his teeth in her face. "Do you want me to slit your throat? Because unless you tell me everything you know about Charlotte Holt, you're dead!"

Knife. He had a knife. The cold prick she felt against her neck was a blade. Jess grabbed for his wrist with both hands, tried to force his hand back. She might as well have been pushing a forklift. "I don't know anything! She left! She's not here!" Jess had no idea whether Charlotte was still home or not -- for all she knew, her roommate was hiding in a closet -- but if this bastard didn't know where she was, Jessica wasn't going to give her away. (*This establishes that Jess is a heroic person willing to sacrifice herself to save her friend. That kind of thing tends to make the reader care about her.*)

* * *

Try to capture the "voice" of the viewpoint character -- the way they think and speak. In the next scene from *Guardian*, I have a fight between Frieka, my cyborg talking wolf, and his fellow warriors. The wolf's computer has been deactivated, and I wanted to show how his thoughts had become non-verbal and simplified. I also wanted to stress the emotion that drives him. The antagonist has arranged for the heroine, Raine, to be trapped in time. Freika wants revenge because he sees her as his child.

* * *

The wolf trailed the thief who'd stolen his child, following the traitor's scent into a familiar room full of tables and people and the rich smell of food.

His enemy sat at a table with the wolf's friends. The child thief had fooled them all, and that made the wolf's simmering rage leap even higher.

He moved across the room in a low, rapid slink, his eyes fixed on the child thief's smug face. The wolf could almost taste the traitor's blood. (*Note the repetition of the phrase "child thief." Normally I avoid repeating words so close together, but here it emphasizes Freika's animal thought patterns. I don't use any names of these characters, because the wolf isn't capable of speech without his computer.*)

He heard one of his friends call his name, but he had no way to answer. And didn't care. All that mattered was killing the child thief.

The wolf did not bother walking around the table. He simply leaped across it, his powerful muscles clearing its width in one easy bound. He slammed into the child thief's chest with his full weight. The thief screamed like a rabbit as his chair went over, dumping him on the floor as the wolf went for his throat.

The thief's arm blocked the way, and the wolf bit. Bone snapped, and the taste of hated blood filled his mouth. Another rabbit scream. People shouted, bellowed the wolf's name. He ignored them and lunged for the child thief's throat again.

Just before his teeth closed, strong hands closed in his ruff and lifted him like a puppy. Threw him halfway across the room. He landed, kept his feet, skidded on the slick floor, then found traction and charged forward again.

Tattooed not-Baran man blocked his way, shouted his name. Must have been the one who'd thrown him. Must have denied him the child thief's life. The wolf lowered his head and snarled a warning.

And leaped for tattooed-man.

* * *

A hundred kilos of pissed-off wolf slammed into Alerio's chest. The Warlord fought not to go down, instead burying his hands in the big beast's ruff. He barely managed to keep those snapping teeth from his throat. "Freika, back off, dammit! Stop!" (*Note that the writing styles of the two points of view are different. You must get into the character's head and decide how they would think and their attitude toward what's happening in the scene. Also keep in mind the character's accent, the jargon they'd use in their profession, their education, etc. Avoid using phonetic spelling to depict an accent because it can be hard to process what the misspelled words mean. Too, those misspellings can make the character seem ignorant and a bit stupid. Instead, I'd use standard spelling and depict the accent with word choice.*)

The wolf's only answer was a ripping snarl, another lunge, and the castanet snap of teeth. Alerio barely forced the wolf's jaws away from his throat.

Galar and three other Enforcers tackled Freika and helped Alerio wrestle him to the floor. The huge animal twisted and fought, snapping, claws ripping through the thin fabric of their uniforms as he scrabbled to escape them.

"Fuck, Chief!" Galar bellowed, slinging a leg across the wolf's back so he could sit on him. "Freika's vocalizer is off!"

"I noticed!" And according to Alerio's sensors, so was the wolf's computer. Which meant all that was left was instinct, rage, and a whole lot of teeth and claws with no interest in listening to reason.

* * *

When you're writing different characters like this, try to imagine how they'd fight, given the abilities they have. In the next sequence, I do battlefield combat *à la Lord of the Rings*. This is from *Master of Dragons* (2007), in which my hero, Kel, is a shapeshifting dragon and my heroine, Nineva, is a Sidhe magic user.

This is also a sample of how I write a battle between armies. Don't focus on troop movements, unless your protagonist is the general in charge of them. The heroic character is the one the readers care about. Keep your focus on them and their struggle to survive.

* * *

She felt his magic flood over her skin, and he was a dragon again. Given the howls and screams coming from the battlefield, Nineva was damned glad of it.

She ran forward, grabbed the harness he wore, and managed to haul herself up and onto his neck. He leaped skyward before she was even settled. Nineva grabbed at the straps, kicked her feet into the stirrups, and held on for dear life.

Kel's huge wings carried them up and over the battle into a sky full of darting, fire-breathing dragons and their warrior passengers. Unfortunately, it was also full of magical blasts, boiling with energy and zipping through the air like anti-aircraft fire.

The blasts were huge, easily the size of boulders, and a seething blood red.

And they stank of death magic.

One ate through one dragon's shield even as he twisted and fought to escape. A heartbeat later, he and his rider burst into flame and fell screaming from the sky. (*The idea here is to make the reader imagine what getting hit by one of these blasts would be like.*)

"Holy fuck," Nineva whispered, chilled to the marrow as she looked away from the impact.

Kel jolted under her. "Arthur!" She had to grab for the harness as he suddenly went into a dive, plummeting toward the ground. She barely managed not to scream as she conjured a crossbow nocked with a magical bolt.

They found Arthur squared off with an enormous Dark One. The alien looked surprisingly like a medieval woodcut of a demon, standing a good nine feet tall on two hooves, its lower body covered with thick black fur. The rest of it was bright red, with huge clawed hands, tusklike teeth jutting from its lower jaw, and a pair of curving black horns. It hacked at Arthur with a huge axe it held in both hands. The axe rang against Excalibur as the alien tried to batter its way through Arthur's guard. (*Normally I keep my paragraphs short in a fight. But this is the first time we see one of these demons up close, so I had to give you a description. I'm trying to scare the reader through Nineva's emotions. How are Nineva and Kel going to survive?*

It had apparently landed at least one good blow. A river of scarlet spilled down the vampire's armored chest as he danced around his foe. It looked like far too much blood to Nineva's healer's eye.

The Dark One looked up and saw Kel plummeting toward him. The creature fired off a spell blast, forcing Kel to jerk to one side. Even as the dragon steadied under her, Nineva took careful aim with her crossbow and fired. Her bolt lodged in the Dark One's massive shoulder, but he brushed it off like a mosquito.

Oh, she thought, *that's not good at all.* (*There's no better way to increase tension than showing the protagonist's attack having no effect. Also, part of Nineva's internal conflict is the fact she's playing way out of her league. This reinforces it. The reader should be afraid for her.*)

Kel slammed into the Dark One like a freight train, knocking the alien off his feet. There was a sickening crunch, and the dragon roared in pain. Nineva conjured another bolt and stood up in her stirrups, trying to see over Kel's massive body. She saw nothing but a blurring impression of a lashing dragon neck and the flash of the Dark One's magical axe. There was no way to get a shot at all. (*If you're fighting from the back of a dragon, you'd have a hard time seeing over the beast's huge neck and head.*

This adds to the sense of fear and vulnerability. We know our hero was hurt, but we don't know how badly.)

"Kel!" she screamed over the howls of combat. "Dammit!" She vaulted from the harness. Landing on her feet, she scuttled around the dragon, narrowly avoiding his swinging tail. (*Make sure you involve your heroine in your fights. Having her stand back and wring her hands is not very heroic.*)

Blood ran down Kel's muzzle from a wound over his eye as he breathed a gout of flame at the Dark One. The blast boiled off the creature's shield with such heat and power, Nineva could feel it from where she stood.

As the flames died, the Dark One charged, drawing back his axe as he aimed for Kel's head.

Nineva fired her crossbow right into the alien's eye. The creature toppled, its body bursting into flame as her spell tore through it.

Stunned, she dropped her crossbow and stared. She hadn't expected that to actually work. (*Since this is part of the climax, I'm building Nineva's confidence so she can defeat her inner conflict.*)

* * *

Now let's look at the techniques you use in constructing fights, beginning with using YouTube to find and research techniques your characters can use to survive.

Chapter Eight: Going Tubing

The first thing you need to consider is where the fight falls in the book and how it will affect the characters and their conflict with the antagonist.

In most of the book, a fight's effect on the protagonists will be negative. They'll lose, they'll get hurt, and there may be legal or financial consequences. They could even be hospitalized, arrested, or sued.

Remember, your objective is to increase the pressure on them to make the reader wonder how they're going to get out of this mess. The harder it is for the characters, the greater the emotional payoff for the reader when they win.

At the same time, fights must escalate, getting more and more nasty.

When you're preparing to write a fight, first determine where it is in the book, the outcome you want, and how it will affect the plot. What do you want this fight to say about your protagonists? How will you use it to illustrate the problems created by their internal conflicts?

Internal conflicts *must* create problems so we'll anticipate the disaster they could cause in the climax. Their psychic wound should act like a set of lead weights on the character's ankles.

For the sake of this exercise, I'm going to assume that this is the book's opening scene. My intent is to establish my protagonist as a formidable fighter, so the reader will anticipate all the trouble he's going to get into.

In a romance, you don't want your male lead to be the stereotypical 98-pound weakling. Now, that may be perfectly fine in other genres, especially if you want to depict a hero's character arc on the way to becoming a badass. It depends on the kind of book you're writing and the market you're writing it for.

But *this* story is a romance, so the hero must be sexy and formidable.

Note that even if the hero wins early fights, his internal conflict must create problems for him. He also must feel pain and fear to jack up the tension for the reader.

If I were writing this book for real, I'd make sure the hero gets his head handed to him in the next scene. If we've set the protagonist up as a skilled and capable fighter, the antagonist's next victory will make the bad guy seem even more intimidating. After all, he's put this badass on the ropes.

If you're writing a romance, you can then use the antagonist to intensify the reader's worry about the heroine. Since she's probably not in the hero's weight class, the reader knows the antagonist is an even greater threat to her.

If you're writing in some other genre, you may still want to put someone the protagonist loves in the line of fire to increase the stakes.

For the purposes of this exercise, I decided to show the protagonist being attacked by multiple opponents. I headed to YouTube to spend several fascinating hours watching videos by various martial artists.

(Mind you, just because someone has a YouTube channel, you can't assume they know what they're talking about. One "instructional" video featured a slap fight between three teenagers. I watched it for ten seconds, snorted, and returned to my search queue.)

The channel I found most useful is called *Fight Science*, presented by Dr. Mark Phillips. His bio describes him as a criminal psychologist, high-risk security consultant, and martial arts and defensive skills instructor. It lists his martial arts disciplines as Wing Chun, Brazilian Jiu Jitsu, Judo, Wrestling, Boxing, San Da Kickboxing, and MMA.

I watched several of Phillips's videos on fighting multiple attackers and handling unexpected street aggression. What he has to say about body language and fight strategy makes sense. I recommend you spend a few hours watching his videos.

Other channels I watched included *Fight Smart Trav* and *FIGHTTIPS*. Those gave me ideas I could use in the beginning and the middle of the fight, but what I really needed was the final blow I could use to end it.

I found one I liked at *Funker Tactical Fight Training Videos* (a channel I've used before) which featured a video called, "The Fred Mastro Handshake."

Fred is a bouncer, and the video demonstrates what he does when a customer gets aggressive. First, he snaps his right hand across to the right side of the guy's face, grabbing his head and holding him still. At the same time, he slams the side of his left fist into man's neck under the ear, disrupting his carotid's blood supply and stunning him.

Fred then grabs the opponent's shoulder, spinning him around and bending him backward over the bouncer's knee so Fred can finish him off. The whole thing takes less than a second.

Now that I look at it, however, I'm not sure Fred's "handshake" is a great move for a fictional fight. It takes so long to describe the attack, it would slow the pacing. Worse, the reader would have a hell of a time visualizing what's going on. A good fictional fight works better with simpler moves, since complex ones can be confusing.

Now, if I were writing an assassin antagonist

ambushing a victim, I might use Fred's Handshake -- it's the kind of thing you do when you intend to kill someone. Since it would be the only move of the fight, the pacing wouldn't matter.

I found a better idea for the start of the fight in a *Fight Science* video called "1 Takes on 3 Like Boss...Teaches Us Lessons in Self Defense." The video is an analysis of Russian CCTV video where a man gets into an argument with three others in an elevator. He starts to leave, then whirls and lays into the trio as they're trapped in the bottleneck of the open elevator doorway. They fall back, stunned, and he lands a flurry of vicious blows before making his escape.

Phillips quoted an old saying as he narrated the video: "Three against one isn't fair to the three." That is, assuming the one can maneuver the three into getting in each other's way.

But Phillips warns that you can't expect to beat up all three opponents -- you're more likely to end up hospitalized or dead. Instead, try to talk your way out of the situation. If that doesn't work, launch a savage attack to create confusion, then run.

Now, you may think running's fine for real life, but is it something you want your heroic protagonist to do? That depends. If he's a Captain America clone, he can hang around and whip everybody into butter. But if he's a plain vanilla human, having him run is smart. He can vow to pick them off one at a time later.

Phillips and Trav agreed the last thing you want to do is let your enemies surround you. If everyone starts pounding on you at once, you're done.

Instead, step back or to the side, forcing them to come at you one at a time until you can create an opportunity to escape. Move constantly as you face your opponents, keeping one between you and the rest at all times. Watch for an escape route, and don't let them encircle you.

To buy an opportunity to escape, pick a victim at one end of the group and grab them by the head or shoulder, yanking them between you and the rest while punching them. Accept the fact that you're going to get hit and probably hurt. Phillips says it can't be avoided, so don't let it stop you.

That's an excellent attitude for your hero. A strong protagonist keeps fighting as long as they're conscious and capable of throwing a punch.

Trav suggests a similar technique for use with multiple opponents called the Muay Thai Clinch. Choose the nearest opponent, hook both hands around the back of their neck, pull their head down, then punch a knee repeatedly into their face and belly.

Meanwhile, keep your captive between you and the rest of the pack. This forces them to punch over their buddy, so they can't strike with as much force. They may even trip over your prisoner's legs. If an attacker tries to come around from the side, you can drive them off with a kick or two.

Phillips, however, doesn't like kicks when facing multiple opponents. Kicks require you to balance on one leg, leaving you off-balance and vulnerable to being tripped. Then they'll all pile on.

However, if you're writing a *fictional* fight, go for it. Have it backfire on your hero and get him beaten up, depending on the needs of your plot.

The question is, how do you capture the guy's head to begin with?

In one *Fight Tips* video, martial artist Shane Fazen and fight choreographer Jeremy Marinas of 87 Eleven demonstrate a similar tactic. Grab an opponent's coat collar, jerk them into a bending position, then yank the coat up around their face so they can't see. You can then whip them around by the collar, keeping them between you and the pack.

The advantage there is that you can stand a little farther back instead of right up in the captive's face, as in the Muay Thai Clinch. This gives you more room to maneuver while aiming disabling kicks at your victim's legs.

Marinas cautioned that most guys aren't going to let you grab their collars, so he suggested going for the hold just before or just after the opponent launches a punch. Duck under the punch and slam into them at the waist. As the guy staggers backward, grab a fistful of coat, then keep him between you and his friends.

A Few More Useful Tips from Fight Science

If an opponent looks around when they're talking to you, Phillips says they're either looking for witnesses or trying to distract you. Either way, a sucker punch may be on the way. That sounds like a great clue to tell your protagonist he's about to get jumped.

You know that saying about watching a person's eyes to see if they're going to attack you? Phillips said don't do that -- "You're not taking them out for dinner and a movie." It's the shoulders that signal when someone is going to attack, since you must rotate the upper body to swing. This is called *telegraphing a punch*.

If the shoulders move but the arm doesn't, they're setting up for a kick.

He recommends you avoid using your own shoulders when you're about to sucker punch someone. Instead, step in close enough to launch the strike from the elbow, rotating the hips into the punch to maximize its power.

Unfortunately, that means you're also close

enough to get sucker punched yourself. Phillips advises you should avoid doing what he calls "the primate dance" -- getting up in your opponent's face, chin up, arms out, in a lousy position to block incoming blows.

Instead, he said to keep your chin down and your eyes up. It gives the impression of confidence. If your opponent does punch you in the face, the blow is more likely to strike the forehead and glance down into the chest, protecting vulnerable facial bones. If they try to headbutt you instead, they'll hit the thicker bones of the forehead instead of the fragile nose and cheekbones.

(That pose is also disturbing as hell. Remember Jack Nicholson in Kubrick's *The Shining*, staring at his wife with his chin angled down and his eyes turned up at her? That was creepier than the twin ghost girls. As a cover artist, I've found posing a hero that way gives him a serial killer vibe, no matter how handsome he is.)

When facing an opponent, bend your knees slightly so you're less vulnerable to being knocked off-balance, and set your feet apart, making it easier to push, pull or drive.

When outnumbered, Phillips suggests taking the fight to your attackers. They won't expect it, and they may not be experienced in fighting in a group. (Fighting effectively as a team -- or against one -- takes practice to do well.) Striking first gives you a narrow window to hurt one of them.

Punch *up* if you're aiming for the cheekbone or the eye socket. You can also use an open hand to protect your knuckles, striking hard with the heel of the palm. Use the edge of the hand to hit the throat, cutting off blood supply or damaging the trachea -- *if* you can justify using lethal force because your life is in danger. You don't want to end up in prison.

Phillips points out that every time you can make an opponent block a punch, they're not attacking. Keep them too busy dealing with *your* blows to launch their own and you'll get hurt less.

Footwork is key in a fight against multiple attackers. Keep moving and pay attention to the environment to make sure you don't trip over a curb or slam into a wall.

At least, that's what you'd do if you were in a real-life fight. As the writer, you may *want* your protagonist to screw up. Have them trip over that curb or back into that wall. It'll give your bad guys an opening you can use to make your character's life miserable -- and wind your reader up.

Watching these videos gave me a better idea how my protagonist would handle the situation -- and how it could blow up in his face.

Now let's write that scene.

Chapter Nine: Fair to the Three

Every first scene has certain jobs, such as establishing who the protagonist is and why we should care about them. It also tells us where and when we are -- a nineteenth-century ballroom, a grimy 21st century alley, the bridge of a starship.

The scene may also lay out the character's internal conflict or psychic wound, if possible. Either way, work to build reader sympathy for the protagonist, especially if they're an antihero the reader might otherwise dislike.

Hate in an Elevator

The elevator fight I researched in the previous chapter proved to be challenging. In part, that's because I decided a simple brawl wasn't a good enough example. Your first fight scene needs to reveal character, establish your antagonists, and elicit reader sympathy for the protagonist.

It also has to seem like something people would actually do. The minute the reader thinks, "Wait, that doesn't make any sense," you've lost them.

I'd intended to write the thug antagonists as muscle sending the hero a message from their boss. Then I realized gang members would be armed. If you've got guns, you don't bother throwing punches. You just shoot the guy.

Wrestling with that, I went for a long walk and started dictating the scene into my phone's recording app. I think better moving, especially when I'm not sure where the scene is going. I'm not alone in this. Studies have found creativity is enhanced by exercise. (Bergland 2012) Sure enough, the fight flowed easily after that.

It also didn't end up quite the way I'd planned.

Here's the first draft. It's rough as hell, but with a first draft, that's good enough. You just want to get the big moves and dialogue beats on the page. None of it needs to be pretty. I'll show you how to clean it up in the next section.

* * *

The minute they walked into the elevator, something about the three men made the hair stand up on James Harper's neck. (*This is the hook -- the very first line of the story. A good hook will make readers buy the book just to find out what's going on. Actually, every scene needs some sort of hook to engage the reader's interest and curiosity. When trying to come up with a hook, look for something that will make the reader ask what's going on. Why did the hair stand up on Harper's neck? Ask yourself what's unusual about this scene? Hint at trouble about to break loose* RIGHT NOW. *Also note that I give the protagonist's full name. You need to do that whenever you introduce an important character.*)

It wasn't a very big elevator to begin with, and it seemed to shrink as the doors closed. (*Enhancing the sense of threat. Also tells us when and where we are, which the reader needs to know. We don't want to give the impression this is taking place in a featureless white room.*)

Afghanistan and Iraq had sharpened Jim's asshole detector, and it started blaring like an airhorn. (*Establishing character. This tells us he's a combat vet, and the phrase "asshole detector" gives an impression of sardonic humor. Readers like funny protagonists -- they're entertaining and surprising. Note I do not then go on to drop three paragraphs about Jim's service in the Marines. That exposition would stop the story in its tracks. Give just enough to tease.)*

"Fifteen, please," one said in a cultured baritone as his buddies blocked the closing elevator doors. No escape there. And this elevator was slow as hell.

Well, fuck. Jim had a meeting with the client in his office in five minutes, but he was probably going to be late -- assuming he got there at all. (*This line is designed to raise questions. Client of what? What does Jim do?*)

All three men wore suits and ties, though two of them looked like pro wrestlers playing dress-up. Probably guns in those suits. Both the wrestlers were taller than Jim, who wasn't exactly a shrimp. (*You want the bad guys to have an obvious physical advantage.*)

They also looked like beating the hell out of people was their chosen career path. And they stared at him with the kind of icy assessment you don't give a stranger unless you're planning to kick his ass.

The balding forty-something ginger looked a little soft around the belly -- could be slow, no endurance, but Jim wouldn't know for sure until the fight started. The second was leaner, a little broader, dark haired, thirty or so. Cold blue sociopath eyes held his as the asshole reached up to scratch a scarred cheek. Had the number 14 crudely tattooed in blue ink on the back of his hand. A white supremacist prison tatt. (*I'm not normally a huge fan of sentence fragments, but here I'm trying to establish Jim's voice and the way adrenaline makes his thoughts race.*)

Shit. Can't get to my shoulder holster with my jacket buttoned. Jim always wore a suit to client appointments. (*Feed little clues to motivate readers to make predictions and look for more information to see if they're right.*)

I'm going to need to distract them while I get to my weapon. (*That line is stilted. Needs a rewrite.*)

The third guy wore a gray pinstriped suit, tailored and expensive. Probably Armani. His artistically graying hair was styled in a precise cut. His long, thoroughly ordinary face would have seemed pleasant if it hadn't been for the reptilian look in his hazel eyes. Jim had testified in enough court cases to know an attorney when he saw one. (*Another hook.*)

That took the threat level down a couple of notches. The protective globe of a security camera bulged on the elevator's ceiling, and the lawyer wasn't going to let his thugs commit murder in front of it. (*Which takes care of the problem of why they don't just shoot him.*)

The lawyer gave him a faint, cold smile. "Mr. Harper?"

Yeah, he hadn't thought this little encounter was a coincidence. "And you are?"

"William Rosen of Rosen, James, and Associates. My client has reason to believe that a member of his family means to hire you. I'd like to fill you in about the situation."

Jim gave him the expressionless gaze he'd learned in boot camp with a Marine DI screaming inches from his face. "Who's your client?"

"Jefferson Tremaine," the lawyer said, in the kind of smug tone flunkies used when saying names like Darth Vader. (*Clunky. Needs a rewrite.*)

"Mr. Tremaine's daughter has unfortunately been diagnosed with bipolar disorder. He is terribly worried she might self-harm."

By committing suicide with a bullet in the back of her skull, Jim thought. No wonder the woman had sounded anxious on the phone.

"He would like to request that if Clarissa contacts you, you give me a call." He reached into his lapel, pulled out a thin gold case, and plucked out a business card. "There's a nice reward in it for you. Ten thousand is a lot more than Clarissa can afford to pay. Especially since her funds have been cut off." (*Another stilted line, but that's what rewrites are for. Just get the raw scene down and worry about fixing it later.*)

"Okay." Jim gave him a casual shrug and took the card, though he'd cut off his own balls before he'd fuck over a client. (*Establishes that yes, this is a man with ethics. However, that line is going to need work. It has nowhere near enough snap.*)

What the hell had Clarissa Tremaine seen that made her own father decide to kill her? (*Hook.*)

The elevator stopped as it reached Jim's floor. The men let him through, and he stepped between them. Maybe he was going to get out of this without a shitstorm IED going off in his face... (*Cue the shitstorm IED.*)

The opening doors framed a slender blond woman, pretty, somewhere around twenty-five. She wore an enormous messenger bag cross-body in front of her, and a pair of black slacks and an emerald silk blouse. (*Awkward sentence. Got to rewrite that.*)

An ugly bruise distorted one high cheekbone. Her gray gaze went to Jim first, then slid to the three men behind him and widened in absolute terror.

Oh fuck.

"Clarissa!" the lawyer snapped.

Prison Tatt lunged toward the door, obviously intending to bull past Jim and grab her. She'd probably commit "suicide" soon afterward.

Jim whirled, driving an uppercut with his full body weight behind it. It slammed into Tatt's chin, snapping his head back. In a continuation of the same motion, Jim whipped his left arm around the guy's neck, jerked Tatt's head down, and powered a knee up into his face. Bone crunched and Tatt howled in outraged pain. (*When you're writing an attack, think where the character's arm is going to be after that punch. Jim's arm is in position to hook the guy's head and jerk it down, where Jim's knee would be. So, knee in the face.*)

"Run!" Jim roared at the girl, not turning to see if she obeyed. (*Fight scenes between people of the same gender can get confusing, because readers don't know which "he" or "him" you're talking about. This forces you to use names to avoid confusing the reader. That's why I give these thugs nicknames, since the lawyer wouldn't introduce his muscle.*)

From the corner of one eye, Jim saw the ginger going for his shoulder holster.

"Not here!" the lawyer snapped. "This is assault, Mr. Harper!"

Fuck off. Tatt slammed a fist into his gut, but Jim had clenched his abdominals, and it didn't do much. (*Got to rewrite that. Jim needs to get hurt.*)

The big man rammed him, trying to shove him over backward. Jim fisted the collar of Tatt's jacket as he backpedaled out of the elevator, jerking the jacket half over the man's head and bending him over further. Kneed him in the face again. This time the screamed curse bubbled.

Ginger lunged at him, and Jim shoved Tatt at him, calculating which way to run. (*And I need to fix that line.*)

He was willing to bet he was faster than either of these two fuckers.

But even as he started to step backward, his back hit something yielding. Before he could whirl, an arm extended past his face. Holding a gun.

A woman's voice said, cold and steady, "That's enough, boys."

The three men in the elevator froze, eyes widening. "You know how good a shot I am," Clarissa Tremaine said in a clear, cold voice. (*Rewrite needed.*)

"And you also know I can shoot all of you before you can draw your weapons." (*Hmmm. Not sure about her word choice there. Would she say weapons?*)

Sounds stilted.)

What the fuck? Jim drew his own gun and leveled it at the three men. "Hands up."

Ginger and Tatt looked furious but sullenly raised their hands. The lawyer wore the panicked expression of someone who knew the situation had spun totally out of control. "No one wants to hurt you," he said in a shaking voice. "You need help."

"Yeah, I know exactly what kind of help you've got in mind. That's why I've got a broken rib."

"I'll cover them," Jim said. "You call the cops."

Her laugh sounded bitter. "My father owns the cops. In fact, you're probably the only man in town he doesn't own. Which is why I need my own muscle." (*Awkward.*)

He felt her move behind him, doing something against his back with one hand as she kept the gun leveled over his shoulder with the other. (*This is both a hook and me dealing with a POV issue. Jim can't see what she's doing, but with her pressed against his back, he'd know it's something. And it also gives me a hook in that the reader is going to wonder what she's up to, given she's already got a gun on the jerks.*)

Then her left hand came up over his shoulder, and from the corner of one eye, he saw a big canister with a pistol grip attached to the top. *The fuck?*

"Go!" she snapped in his ear and pulled the trigger. He ducked under her arm, getting out of the way as she started hosing the men down with a tight, reeking stream of pepper spray. They howled and cursed, choking as it splashed into their faces.

As the elevator doors closed, he stared at her. She must have had the canister, like the gun, in the messenger bag. "Where the fuck did you get riot control spray? That's not even legal for civilian use."

She shrugged. "I'm a Tremaine. Let's get the fuck out of here before Rosen calls reinforcements."

And they ran for the stairs.

* * *

That was *not* how I'd planned that fight to go. I'd figured Jim would use the Fred Mastro Handshake to take out the lawyer. Trouble is, that would only make the thugs more determined to kill Jim, since Rosen signs their checks.

So how was I going to give the protagonists an opportunity to get away?

And why wouldn't Jim and Clarissa simply call the cops once they'd gotten the drop on the thugs? You can't have your protagonists ignore an obvious solution. Either they try it, and it backfires, or you come up with a reason it won't work. In this case, I made the cops crooks, which also explains why Clarissa didn't go to the police to begin with.

I'd seen video of police using that riot control spray, and I thought it would be the perfect way to give the protagonists a chance to escape. Regular pepper spray is nasty, but people can ignore it if they're motivated enough. Getting shot in the face with a stream of riot control spray would probably put anyone down for ten or fifteen minutes.

Jim would have no reason to carry something

like that, though. Clarissa does, given that she's badly outnumbered and hunted by murderous creeps.

What's more, the fact that she *does* carry it reveals what kind of person she is. She also comes off as ruthless, which makes her interesting. Likewise, it suggests a romantic conflict, because Jim's an idealist, and she, just as obviously, is not.

The other interesting thing about this scene is that it will get the protagonists into serious trouble. There's a camera in the elevator, and security video doesn't usually have audio. It would look as if Jim assaulted those men, and Clarissa doused them with an illegal weapon. Rosen and Tremaine would spin the situation to make the two look like criminals.

That's exactly what I'd want in a real book. Every fight scene should make the situation worse for your characters, even when they appear to win.

You may have noticed that Jim and Clarissa make short work of the bad guys, which doesn't follow my dictate that the bad guys should usually win early in the book. However, this is the inciting incident that kicks off the story as the antagonists make their first move.

Inciting incidents establish A) why the reader should care about the protagonist, and B) that the hero really is heroic. My protagonists usually do well in those first fights. It's the later brawls -- at the midpoint and three-quarters point -- where the antagonists rack up the score. Or, if you need the good guys to win for plot purposes, they end up handing the bad guys a weapon the antagonists can use against them.

However, the scene still has some serious flaws I need to fix. Lots of awkward sentences, not enough sensory description to pull the reader into the scene, and no sign of Jim's internal conflict. I don't want to go into detail about what it is -- that could bog down the book with backstory -- but I do need to hint at it. Here's the rewrite, with the changes in bold.

* * *

It wasn't a very big elevator to begin with, **and it seemed to shrink as the men entered. James Harper eyed the three as his asshole detector blared like an airhorn**. (*Cut unnecessary words where possible. Tight sentences are clearer. Longer sentences act like speed bumps -- not what you want when the action is fast. I moved the line about the asshole detector to compress and smooth the paragraph. I also cut the reference to Afghanistan and Iraq. It's redundant given the paragraph below.*)

His heart began to pound, rabbiting in his chest, filling his ears with thunder. Sweat rolled down his back. Fighting the adrenaline dump, he began to breathe in through his nose, out through his mouth, deeply, forcing his heartbeat to slow. *This is no time for a flashback.*

That goddamn alley in Dahaneh **was eleven years ago. He should be over this shit by now.** (*And there's his internal conflict. Note I don't tell you that Dahaneh was a battle the US Marines fought in Afghanistan in Helmand Provence in 2009. You don't need to know yet, and I want to make you wonder. I started to cut the line about the elevator being small, but then I realized it made a better hook than what I'd had in mind.*)

"Fifteen, please," one said in a cultured baritone as his buddies blocked the closing doors. (*This explains why Jim doesn't just leave the elevator.*)

No escape there. And this elevator was slow as

hell. *Well, fuck.* Jim had a meeting with a client in five minutes. He'd be late -- assuming he got there at all. (*I cut the original line in two to improve flow. Also, I'm trying to establish he's got damned good instincts.*)

Grimly, he hit fifteen.

As the elevator lurched and creaked upward, Jim eyed the three. His heartrate had dropped to normal as the threat of the flashback receded.

They wore suits and ties, **though two of them looked like cosplaying pro wrestlers.** Bet they had weapons concealed somewhere. (*Cleaning up an awkward line.*)

Both WWE dickheads were taller than Jim, who wasn't exactly a hobbit. (*Changed the wording to give the line more snap. "Shrimp" is a cliché.*)

They also looked like beating hell out of people was a job that gave them joy. And they were staring at him with the kind of icy assessment you didn't give a stranger unless **you were** planning to kick his ass.

The balding forty-something ginger looked a little soft around the belly -- could be slow, no endurance, but Jim wouldn't know for sure **unless** a fight started. The second was leaner, a little broader, dark haired, thirty or so. **Emotionless shark eyes held his as the asshole reached up to scratch a scarred cheek. 14 was crudely tattooed in blue ink across the back of his hand.**

Prison tatt. *Great.*

Their suit jackets were unbuttoned. *They're*

definitely packing. Shit. Can't draw my gun with my jacket buttoned. Jim always wore a suit to client appointments. **He'd have to distract them while he unbuttoned it.**

His heartbeat started accelerating again, and he went back to combat breathing. *Steady. Steady. I've been in worse situations.* (*Which should tell you something about him right there.*)

The third guy wore a gray pinstriped suit, tailored and expensive. Probably Armani. His artistically graying hair was styled in a **precision** cut, **and his long face looked pleasantly ordinary until you noticed the reptilian chill in his hazel eyes**. (*"Look" is emotionally neutral. Reptilian chill has more punch. Also improved the flow and got rid of some repetition.*)

Jim had testified in enough court cases to know an attorney when he saw one. That took the threat level down a couple of notches. The protective housing of a security camera bulged on the elevator's ceiling, and the lawyer wasn't going to let his thugs commit murder in front of it.

Pinstripe gave him a faint, icy smile. (*Avoiding the repetition of lawyer. Repetition draws attention to itself and tends to be jarring.*)

"Mr. Harper?"

"And you are?"

"William Rosen of Rosen, James, and Associates. My client has reason to believe that a member of his family means to hire you. **I'd like to caution you about the situation.**"

The elevator creaked in the silence as the tension ratcheted up again. (*I could have used "hummed," but creaked creates a better sense of threat.*)

Another bead of sweat rolled down Jim's spine. He gave Rosen the expressionless gaze he'd learned in boot camp from Marine DIs bellowing in his face. (*Tightened that line to get rid of "inches from his face," and chose a stronger word than screamed. And now we know he's an ex-Marine.*)

"Who's your client?"

"Jefferson Tremaine." The lawyer smiled, smug as an Empire flunky saying "Darth Vader." (*Not sure about that line, though it might work as a character detail. You wouldn't expect Star Wars nerdery of a Special Forces badass.*)

"Mr. Tremaine's daughter has unfortunately been diagnosed as bipolar. He is terribly worried she might self-harm."

By committing suicide with a bullet in the back of her skull. No wonder the woman had sounded anxious on the phone. (*I cut "Jim thought." Didn't need it, and the paragraph flows better without it. I don't use tags like "said" if I can describe the character doing something while they're talking. That serves the same purpose as a tag.*)

"He would like to request that if Clarissa contacts you, you give me a call." Rosen reached into his lapel for a thin gold case and plucked out a business card. "He's offering a $10,000 reward." (*This is the kind of guy who'd use a euphemism when what he means is "bribe."*)

"That's far more than Clarissa can afford. Especially since she no longer has access to her accounts."

"Well, in that case...." Jim faked a casual shrug and took the card, though he'd **chew** off his own balls before he'd fuck over a client. *What the hell did Clarissa see, anyway?*

The elevator slowed to a stop as it **finally, finally** reached Jim's floor. The men stepped to either side **to let him leave, and he moved cautiously between them.** Maybe he was going to get out of this without a shitstorm IED going off in his...

The opening doors revealed a slender blond woman walking past. She broke step and turned toward the elevator, frowning. Pretty, somewhere around twenty-five, dressed in black slacks, an emerald silk blouse, and low-heeled shoes. An enormous Hermes messenger bag hung diagonally across her chest like a shield. The bruise that distorted one high cheekbone was fresh and purple. (*Added some details. It had seemed contrived to me that she was just standing in front of the elevator when it opened. I decided she'd just come up the stairs.*)

Her gray gaze went to Jim first, then slid to the three men behind him... and widened. (*I cut the line about her looking terrified. As a mobster's kid, she wouldn't show fear, whether she felt it or not.*)

Oh fuck.

"Clarissa!" the lawyer snapped.

Prison Tatt lunged toward the door, obviously

intending to **charge** past Jim and grab the girl. Who would probably "commit suicide" **within the hour.**

Jim whirled, driving an uppercut into the thug's chin. As he staggered, Jim whipped his arm around Tatt's neck, jerking his head down and simultaneously slamming a knee up into the asshole's nose. Bone crunched as Tatt howled in outraged pain. (*Though I normally avoid repetition -- all those Jims -- when I'm doing a fight scene with a bunch of men, the choice is between repetition and a confused reader. Confusing the reader is always worse.*)

"Run!" Jim roared at the girl, **struggling to control Tatt as his balding ginger buddy went for a gun. The closing elevator doors hit one of Jim's feet and bounced open again.**

"There's a camera, idiot!" the lawyer barked at Ginger, grabbing his forearm before he could draw. "This is assault, Mr. Harper!"

Still bent, Tatt slammed a fist into Jim's gut. Pain exploded in his ribs as the big man tried to shove him over backward into the hall. Jesus, he was strong. Jim fisted the collar of Tatt's suit coat and stepped back, jerking the jacket half over the thug's head and dragging him into a deeper bow. **He slammed his knee into Tatt's face again just on general principles.** This time the screamed **curse bubbled with blood.**

"You fucker!" Ginger howled, one fist going back as he bulled forward, the lawyer right behind him. Jim shoved Tatt into them. All three men fell in a heap, cursing. Backing away, Jim felt the elevator doors try to close on his

shoulders as he calculated which way to run. Hope he was faster than these...

His back hit something yielding. A feminine hand darted over his right shoulder as the trio scrambled to their feet. From the corner of one eye, Jim saw she held a gun. (*I made some cuts to smooth the action and make it flow faster.*)

Clarissa Tremaine snapped, "That's enough!"

The three men froze, eyes widening. So did Jim -- in sheer, stunned surprise. He could feel the woman standing plastered against him, probably up on her toes to shoot over his shoulder.

"You know I'm an excellent shot," she said icily, "And you also know I'd love a little payback. Hands up."

Now that he had the opportunity, Jim drew his own S&K from his belt holster and leveled it at the men. "You heard her."

Ginger and Tatt looked furious but sullenly raised their hands. The lawyer wore the panicked expression of someone watching a situation spin out of control. "No one wants to hurt you," **Rosen** said in a shaking voice. "You need help."

"Yeah, that rib you broke loves to remind me how much I enjoyed your 'help.'"

She stood utterly still behind Jim, steady as a brick wall. *Damn, girl.* "I'll cover them," he told her in a low voice. "You call the cops."

Her laugh sounded bitter. "My father owns the cops. In fact, you're probably the only man in town he doesn't own... **Pull that gun and you're dead, asshole."** (*Added that one because it didn't seem realistic that the thugs would just stand there with their thumbs up their butts.*)

Still holding the gun braced across his right shoulder, she did something against his back with the other. Reaching into the messenger bag? Something rattled, creaked, rustled. (*Adding sensory detail and clarifying the action.*)

What the hell is she doing? We need to get out of here!

Rosen licked his lips. "Clarissa, your father only wants what's best for..."

"Fuck off." Her free hand slid across Jim's left shoulder, mirroring the one that held the gun over his right. Something hard rapped his chest. From the corner of one eye, he saw she held a big canister by the pistol grip jutting from its cap. *The hell?*

"What are you..." the lawyer began.

"Go!" she snapped in Jim's **ear and pulled the canister's trigger, still holding the gun pointed at the three.**

He ducked under her arm and out of the way as she hosed the men down with a tight, reeking stream of pepper spray.

They recoiled, screaming in startled pain as the burning fluid seared their eyes and open mouths. In seconds, they wouldn't be able to see, much less breathe.

"Cuuunt!" Tatt roared over the canister's hiss. "I'm going to..."

"Clarissa, you fucking bitch!" Rosen howled.

"Back at you!" she yelled, pulling her arms back and letting the elevator doors close as the men flailed blindly.

Jim coughed as the backwash stung his own nose, staring in admiration as she calmly slid her gun and cannister back into the messenger bag. (*Added some sensory details. Even if the capsicum isn't fired at you, the back spray is going to make you choke.*)

"Where the hell did you get riot control spray? That's not even legal."

Clarissa shrugged. "I'm a Tremaine. Let's get out of here before Rosen calls reinforcements."

And they ran for the stairs.

* * *

You can see how sensory detail, emotion, and dialogue add to the impact, realism, and tension of a scene. Think about what you'd do if you were these characters and make sure they do it.

Try to account for the environment too. For example, I had to work to explain why the elevator doors didn't close, so I had Jim keep getting in the way. Four men fighting in a small elevator doesn't make for a lot of room.

Which brings me to the topic of setting.

Chapter Ten: Setting as Opponent

I should probably begin by saying you're not *required* to have everybody throwing punches. Characters don't usually get physical in genres like regency romances, rom-coms, women's fiction, or the kind of book where the main conflict is between a CEO and his Board of Directors.

But personally, I love me some mayhem. Fights provide sturdy tentpoles I can drape my plot over. Nothing prevents sagging middle disease like a good brawl.

Say you're a discovery writer -- also known as pantser -- at a loss for what comes next. A fight will fix that right up, assuming you make sure it's a believable thing for the characters to do. Fights tend to have serious consequences, and it usually takes intense emotions to make people lose their minds enough to risk the fallout. Nobody threatens death over a botched perm. They just don't go back to that salon.

Not that you should just throw in a fight at random. As we've seen, they're major events with real consequences for both protagonist and antagonist. That's why you should plan your fights carefully, giving a lot of thought to when they occur, why they occur, where they occur, and what consequences they'll have.

Personally, I plan for a fight every 100 pages or so, depending on the length of the book. My novels run about 400 pages, so I have four fights: one in the first two or three chapters, another around page 100, and a third around page 200. Then I start setting up for the climax at 350.

The first one, like my elevator brawl, may be a minor event that just announces somebody nasty is in stirring up trouble. Protagonists are minding their own business until the antagonist forces them into action.

The scene with the assassin bomber at the start of *Master of Fire* is a good example of that kind of inciting incident. There's a sense of growing danger to the scene -- something bad is going to happen -- but Giada manages to defuse the situation. But I also make it clear that she hasn't won -- she's just pissed the bomber off, and he's going to do something even worse as a result.

When I plotted *Master of Fire*, I'd intended that the midpoint fight would be the antagonists threatening to blow up a high school auditorium full of students and parents.

I quickly realized that incident wouldn't work for Chapter Ten. Anything that involves that much potential loss of life should be the climax, so that's where I moved it. (Though I turned the school into a funeral home, which made more sense in the plot.)

Had I done that scene where I'd intended, I would have risked an anticlimax: ending the book with an incident that wasn't as powerful as something in the middle. Each confrontation must build the stakes, with a higher potential body count, injuries, property damage, etc. If you put in something too big too early, you can't top it. In other words, don't set off the atomic bomb in Chapter Two. (Well, unless you're writing a dystopian novel, and the bomb is an inciting incident rather than fight scene.)

One way to raise the stakes of a fight is the presence of lots of potential victims, as in *Master of Fire*. I set up the last fight in the funeral home where several hundred deputies had gathered to mourn a cop killed in an earlier fight. The bomber puts two suicide vests on the sheriff's grandchildren, whom the werewolves had kidnapped, and sends them into the mortuary.

Giada discovers she can't use magic to defuse the vests because there's a spell on them. (Which is me plugging a plot hole.) Logan and another bomb tech must disable them without getting the kids killed.

One of the children tells Giada that there are werewolves in the funeral home. Giada must fight them to keep them from killing the humans while Logan and his partner defuse the suicide vests. If either Giada or Logan fail, the children and a whole bunch of cops will die.

The setting itself can also serve as another opponent in the fight, giving the protagonists something else to overcome. It can also provide elements the characters can use against each other to gain an advantage.

Jim's elevator fight would have ended much differently if it had taken place in a high school gym. The bad guys could have avoided getting sprayed, for one thing. As it was, they couldn't get away.

Scene of the Crime

Whenever you're planning a fight, think about potential locations. Consider the visuals and complications each location offers. Every time you can make a bad situation worse, do it. The complication will build tension -- and the ultimate dopamine reward for the reader.

For example, let's take a duel at night in the woods. A human fighter is going to be at a serious disadvantage because they can't see a damn thing, and there are all kinds of stuff to trip over. If I'm trying to make matters worse -- and I always do -- the antagonist can see in the dark. Now your protagonist really has problems.

However, sometimes an idea that sounds terrific

turns out to be unworkable. I tried to set a fight in pitch-black woods for *Arcane Betrayal* (2023), but I just couldn't get it to work.

The book's hero, Grant Sawyer, is a police chief. Three Russian assassins are after him. One has a bond with a magical tiger spirit, another is a witch, and the third can cast spells by singing. Grant's a plain vanilla human cop, so he's seriously outgunned.

To brainstorm the scene, I headed into my neighborhood woods to think it through.

I soon realized I couldn't come up with a way for Grant to win. All that underbrush meant that in darkness, he'd stumble into every briar patch. Then there's the Russians' magical abilities, which would allow them to see him when he can't see them. The odds were *too* stacked against him for him to believably win -- or even survive.

I could have done it *unbelievably*, of course, but that's called giving a character plot armor, and it irritates the crap out of readers.

I finally had to move the fight to the middle of the small town where he's police chief. Then I gave him an AR-15 so the guy with the tiger couldn't eat him.

Now, Grant's heroine, Margay Whitfield, is a Feral with her own magical bond to a tiger spirit, so she could hold her own with the bad guys. But if Margay were on the scene, she'd fight the other Talents while Grant stood around trying not to get killed. Never do that to a protagonist. Both characters *must* play a role in beating the Big Bad.

I needed her down and out for a while, so I had the villains ram the couple's car, trapping Margay in the wreckage. Since she's out cold and the tiger Feral is talking about eating her, Grant decides to lure the antagonists away.

Protagonists should *always* rescue themselves in the climax. If someone else -- like the cops -- saves them during the final fight, you've just given your book an anticlimax.

Planning and Escalating Fights

When I'm planning a big fight, I often spend a week just walking around thinking about it. You want to tailor the fight in such a way that it forces the protagonist to confront their vulnerabilities. Note -- If you have the protagonists win early fights, their opponents should be flunkies rather than the Big Bad. You need to save your primary antagonist for the climax. That way the lead villain can have all kinds of abilities the earlier guys didn't. But make sure he had a reason not to show up for those earlier fights. Maybe he's working on some other part of his plot until he gets sick of the protagonists pummeling his henchmen. Then he can beat the living hell out of your protagonists until they pull off a miracle in the Dark Moment.

Consider the Effect of Each Fight on Your Plot

As you brainstorm the fights leading to the climax, consider the fallout of each. If innocent people are killed, what effect will that have on your protagonist? Will they get into legal trouble? Could they be charged with assault? Is there so much property damage they could get sued? You may want some of that to happen. In *Arcane Betrayal*, Grant almost gets himself fired after battling the Russians, since they shot up Main Street.

Say one of your protagonists goes to jail. Does the antagonist use the opportunity to go after the other? (I'd have the target be whoever's physically the weaker of the pair.) Does the jailed protagonist go out of their mind with worry, knowing the villain will go after their loved one?

You bet your laptop.

Remember that the antagonist doesn't get everything *they* want either, which is the protagonist's death. So how is the antagonist going to react? Maybe they become even more determined to kill the protagonist. Maybe the bad guy goes out and finds allies, so our protagonist's situation gets even worse.

If this is a romance, how will the fight affect the relationship between the heroic couple? Chances are one or both of them almost died during this confrontation. How will they react?

That's why I use big fights as turning points in the book's romance. After coming so close to losing each other, the couple realizes the depth of their feelings. Maybe they'll go to bed for the first time or admit they're falling in love.

If you're *not* writing a romance, how does the close call affect the protagonist and their allies? What conflicts does it create? What guilt does it trigger?

The protagonists may have suffered ugly losses in this nasty little brawl. They're going to want revenge. Wring every bit of drama and emotion out of the situation -- injuries, property damage, broken laws, the reactions of friends and family, etc. Think about the real-world implications of your brawl and use them to make life hell for your characters. It will make your world seem more real.

(Remember the first *Avengers* movie, when the alien creatures and the Avengers wrecked midtown Manhattan? In real life, New York would have sued Tony Stark's armor off.)

One caution, though. As you depict the plot's escalating violence, be aware that what you can get away with depends on the market you're writing for. Horror readers can take a lot more gore than would be permissible in a YA, for instance.

But how do you calibrate the degree of mayhem for your audience?

Chapter Eleven: Rated OMG

During fights, people get hurt, often badly. How you depict those injuries depends on the genre.

You can get gory in horror, science fiction, mystery, and espionage. However, if you're writing for children, you absolutely must avoid getting too graphic. Books get banned for that.

If the genre has a primarily female audience, the level of acceptable blood and guts varies. My paranormals and futuristics have a strong action component involving swords and axes, which means serious injuries. Still, I don't want my books to read like Torture Porn. Many romance readers don't want quite that much realism.

However, it depends on the subgenre. In a contemporary romantic comedy, gore isn't appropriate at all. For one thing, there's nothing funny about real suffering. Yet in Motorcycle Club (MC) romances -- which revolve around outlaw biker gangs -- a common trope deals with heroes outright *torturing* someone who hurt the heroine. Some of those scenes are a bit much even for me -- and I've written books with vampire knights beheading people.

You can also get bloody in medieval historical romances, since readers know it was a violent period. Not so much in Regency-set romances where the focus is on manners and society.

Presumably you read the kind of book you're trying to write. Never attempt a genre just because you think it would be easier to sell. Readers will be able to sense how you feel about the material, and they won't be charmed by your attitude. (Which is why I don't write MCs, despite their popularity.) Too, writing something you're not into makes the process harder.

You're going to be spending months, maybe even years, working on this book. You don't want it to be a chore.

Whatever the genre, look at the fight scenes in similar books and use them as a yardstick. If you're still not sure how much you can get away with, write the scene for maximum punch and passion. Submit it and let the editor make the call. It's better to craft a fight that's dramatic and exciting rather than too tame. Your editor will rein you in if you go too far. (By the way, that's the same advice I give when it comes to love scenes.)

There are a couple of ingredients that contribute to how violent -- and exciting -- a scene is.

One is length. Five manuscript pages is the minimum for an early fight. Your readers need time to get into the scene and get their adrenaline flowing. You can't get them charged up in two pages. Any *less* than two pages has zero emotional impact, so an important scene -- of any kind -- needs to be longer.

Now, if your protagonist gets ambushed by the bad guy and knocked unconscious, that's probably a short sequence. You want the scene to be surprising and abrupt, because that's how it feels to the character.

My fights usually run about ten pages. For a climactic battle, I write at least twenty to make damn sure I don't end up with an anticlimax. In fact, I usually spend a couple of chapters on the climax, between the build up to the scene and its aftermath.

Another factor in the level of violence is the amount of gore you depict in your descriptions of injuries. It may be historically accurate in a medieval to show a disemboweled warrior with his intestines lying around him like rolls of red sausage, but I would recommend against it in a romance. (Again, in science fiction or horror, you're good to go.)

You can decrease the gore by glossing over the description. For example, make a flat statement like "he'd been disemboweled," and let the reader imagine the results. While I usually advise writers to describe the smells, tastes, sounds, and textures of a scene, I wouldn't do that with a horrific injury, especially in something like a young adult novel. It would be too much.

When writing a truly bloody scene, I may show how another character reacts to it. In *Jane's Warlord* (2004), the antagonist, Druas, is a time-traveling cyborg who is the real Jack the Ripper. (There was no Victorian Jack in my world. He was never caught because he jumped to the twenty-first century to murder more women there.) He committed his crimes and recorded them to sell to a network of sadistic subscribers as the ultimate snuff porn.

The real Jack's crimes are stomach-churning. The Victorian crime scene photos are nightmarish even in grainy, blurry black-and-white. Since I tell the reader that Druas records the images through his own eyes, I need to show one of those murders.

Whenever an event has major emotional impacts on the characters, it needs to take place on the page. Otherwise, readers will feel cheated. They want to see how the characters react to the event, especially if it's something traumatic.

Yes, this can be intimidating to write, especially if you don't have confidence in your ability to pull the scene off. But the only way you'll learn how to do it is to do it. Every time you tackle a scene that scares the hell out of you, you get better as a writer.

The hero of the book is Baran, a genetically engineered warrior -- or "Warlord" -- whose partner is a talking cyborg wolf. Baran knows a small-town reporter named Jane Colby will be one of Druas's targets, so he shows up at her house to protect her. She's just gotten back from covering the brutal murder of one of Druas's victims, so you can imagine her reaction to finding a wolf and a giant tattooed burglar in her bedroom.

When he tells her she's a target, she demands to see his proof.

* * *

Two minutes into the rest of the recording, Jane bitterly wished she hadn't insisted on seeing it. She forced herself to endure anyway.

At first, she tried to pretend it was some poorly made B-movie she had to review. But no director would have kept the camera focused on what Druas did to Mary Kelly. She'd seen cows butchered with less vicious brutality. (*Technically, this is telling, rather than showing, which you're not supposed to do. But in this situation, I don't want to show it. The things Jack the Ripper did to his victims would have been far too much for romance readers in 2004. Too, this was my very first published novel. You don't want to spring something like that on readers who don't know your work. But I couldn't wimp out with it either.*)

Out of sheer self-defense, she tried to think like a cop, noting which hand he used and how deeply he cut. She wasn't a forensic scientist, but it was obvious from the easy way he hacked into the body that the man's strength was terrifying.

Yet no matter how Jane fought to stay detached, her stomach heaved with every slice. Her head began to pound in deep, rhythmic surges in time to her heart. (*This shows the intensity of her horror and fear. Since readers read for emotion as much as anything else, this keeps the scene powerful, despite the lack of sensory detail.*)

She felt dizzy. Locking her spine into a rigid column, she concentrated on staying upright.

Every time Druas did something particularly nauseating, Jane was conscious of the cool, assessing gazes of Baran and the wolf. *They're wondering how long it will take me to pass out. (Her fight to stay on her feet is her internal conflict for the scene. It also reveals her courage and pride.*)

As the endless seconds ticked past, Jane realized that watching this would leave scars she would carry in her mind until the day she died.

It was only when Druas started cutting Mary's heart out that she jumped up and whirled away. "When you catch this guy…." She had to stop to swallow bile. "Are you going to kill him, or just arrest him?"

"I'm going to kill him." Baran spoke with such utter emotionless conviction, she knew he meant every word.

Jane took a deep breath. "Good." (*Druas's crime is so horrific, Jane believes killing him is the only acceptable outcome.*)

Psychopaths At Play

You do need to show some level of violent description when it comes to the antagonist's actions.

You can't just tell the reader, "Lex Luthor is a vicious, evil genius." You need to show Lex *being* a vicious, evil genius. You want the reader to worry about your protagonist, so don't be too delicate about the antagonist's crimes.

One trick is to reveal the callousness of the character. For example, I describe Druas as humming "Sweet Violets" as he butchers Mary Kelly in the recording. (Sweet Violets" was a popular song at the time that the real-life Mary was heard singing the night she died.) The combination of humming in pleasure and committing a hideous crime highlights how alien this guy is.

Another trick is ending the scene before the villain starts on the victim. Show just enough to give the reader a chill of horror, then cut to the protagonists standing over the body.

This technique is best used when showing the antagonist killing an innocent victim. If they're attacking the heroine or hero -- especially in the climactic fight -- do *not* cut away. The reader knows that the protagonists will survive, especially in a romance. Since the protagonist gives as good as they get, it's not like reading about the torture and murder of a helpless person. Again, the reader wants to share the protagonist's struggle -- and resulting dopamine surge.

When you set up a major incident, pay it off in as much detail as possible. If you get readers worked up with anticipation and don't deliver on your promises, you're going to seriously piss them off. They'll never buy your books again.

I once read a comic book series in which the heroine was methodically tormented by the villain. Toward the end of the series, she gains incredible powers and sets out to get her revenge. I was really looking forward to the next issue, because I wanted to watch her kick the guy's ass. I bought that comic with great anticipation. On the first page, I was furious to learn that the book began *after* that climactic brawl.

The heroine's husband asks, "So what did you do to him?" And the heroine replies, "You don't want to know."

I literally screamed in frustration. That idiot writer had been building to that stupid fight for *six months*. Six months of waiting for that ass-kicking! And he gave me nothing. It's been decades, and I'm still pissed.

Do not do that. Ever.

Paying the Price

In the climax, the protagonists need to really suffer for their victory. If they walk out of the climax without a scratch, your reader will feel they haven't earned their happy ending.

It's all a necessary part of increasing the pressure on your protagonist -- and making your reader sweat.

Now let's look at editing your book for clarity and flow.

Chapter Twelve: Sharpening Your Weapons

Good writing should flow like music, with a rhythm that picks the reader up and sweeps them into the world you've created. Anything that acts like a speed bump needs to go.

Avoid using a bunch of multi-syllable words in a row. I'm not saying you shouldn't use long words -- especially if they have the impact you want -- but use them with restraint. Your job is to tell a story, not impress readers with your vocabulary.

Likewise, trim and rewrite overly complicated sentences. If it has a string of commas and a bunch of clauses, simplify it. Anything readers must stop and decode throws them out of the story. Do that too many times and they'll go find something else to do. And they will never come back. Worse, you will never sell another book to them.

Massaging a Mess

Here's the first paragraph of a rough draft flashback from *Wildcard*, the first book in the *Mothership's Rangers* series. The series deals with genetically engineered warriors who work for an alien ship called *Mothership* in its efforts to prevent human extinction. Despite the futuristic alien tech, the story is set in the present day.

Two of *Mothership*'s warriors are Indra Fox and Diana Newman, who are hunting Satan's Horsemen, a gang of mercenary drug dealers who murdered their parents. Diana and Indra believe they're aliens, since their parents were killed before they had a chance to tell them about *Mothership*.

We lay on the warehouse roof. It was a cloudy

night, and so pitch black, I was glad for my alien eyesight. Not exactly X-ray vision, but it would do. Besides, the utter darkness would make it harder for the Horsemen to spot our silhouettes against the night sky.

As a lead-in to a major scene, the writing's pretty flat, without the emotion and sensory detail to make the scene snap. I also need to identify where the scene takes place. Here's the final draft version:

Diana and I lay on the warehouse roof side by side, cuddling a pair of sniper rifles. It was a cloudy night in Atlanta, with the few streetlamps in the industrial zone either broken or burned out. Either way I was glad for my alien eyesight. Not exactly X-ray vision, but it would do. Besides, the darkness would make it that much harder for the Horsemen to spot our silhouettes against the night sky.

"Cuddling a pair of sniper rifles" is a much better hook than "We lay on the warehouse roof." When you're trying to come up with a hook, think where the characters are and what they're doing. They've got sniper rifles -- they're planning to kill some drug dealers. I thought about the way snipers lie wrapped around their weapons and came up with "cuddling." That's a great verb because it's not something you'd expect people to do with a gun. It also reveals something about Indra's attitude toward what they're doing. Given these are two twenty-year-old girls, the whole bit is unexpected.

Always ask yourself, "How can I make this scene

surprising? How can I put a new twist on it?

As I've said, that kind of cleanup isn't the sort of work you do in the first draft. That one is strictly for getting the action down on the page, even if it's a mess when it gets there.

After that, you'll need at least two more drafts to fix all the vague, clunky, confusing writing. That's not negotiable. *If you're not willing to put in the effort to perfect your work, you're not going to succeed as a writer.*

Second drafts are when I like to add sensory details and description, complicate fight choreography by adding new moves, and intensify interpersonal conflicts between characters.

In the third draft, I clean up the writing to make sure the action is as clear and visual as possible.

I also have critique partners who read my work, just as I read theirs. If they spot something that needs work, I make those edits before submitting the book to my editor. Between her edits and a final round to search for typos, all my books get five to six drafts. The pauses while the book goes back and forth between my editor and me provides me with an opportunity to look at it with fresh eyes.

If you want to be a professional writer, editing is the secret sauce. You must be ruthless with your work. Look at every sentence and ask, "Can I clarify this? Can I give it greater impact?" This is vital no matter how many years you've been writing.

I once had to send a copy of one of my e-books to a reader. I downloaded it from Amazon and read it -- and to my horror, discovered that it was riddled with typos. I have no idea what happened, because I know we edited the final version twice, then ran it through two proofers at minimum. Perhaps somebody uploaded the wrong draft. My publisher and I are fanatical about making sure books are as clean as possible.

Ultimately, though, it was my fault because I didn't reread the book before it went live. My editor and I spent the next two days sending the book back and forth cleaning it up *again*.

That said, you can edit a book to death. I try not to start editing before I finish the first draft. (I do make an exception to that rule when the book goes off the rails and I must figure out what went wrong.)

I have good reasons for that rule.

I decided I wanted to be a writer when I was nine, but I was forty before I completed my first novel. Yet I started actively trying to write a novel when I was in the seventh grade. I began countless novels, yet I never finished any of them until the 1990s *Secrets* novellas. Instead, I'd write chapter one and edit it over and over and *over* until I got sick of it. Don't do that. **Finish the book first!**

Sometimes I still go overboard. My editor once sent a book back to me after the editing was supposedly finished. I read over it -- and found four or five more things I wanted to fix. When I sent it back to the editor, she wrote back, "Stop it! You're obsessing! I wasn't sending it to you to edit."

Ooops.

* * *

Something that's particularly easy to screw up are the fight scenes. In the editing process, you can rewrite a sentence without realizing that the character's arms or legs aren't in position for the attack you have in mind.

It's easy to lose track of where body parts are supposed to be. I've even made similar mistakes writing love scenes. I've had to rewrite a scene when my editor pointed out the character's penis would have to be two feet long for that position to work.

Doing this kind of editing is time consuming, and the first time you must take a machete to your writing can be discouraging. Yet once you see the kind of mistakes you make and figure out how to fix them, you can apply those lessons to your next book.

Writing is one profession in which being an old lady is an advantage. My craft is far better now than it was when I started out. For example, the original version of this book had several scenes from *Jane's Warlord*. But as I edited them for this release, I realized those fights were weaker than scenes in my more recent novels. I cut most of the *Jane* scenes and used *Master of Honor* instead.

That's not to say my work is now perfect by any means. One critique partner pointed out that while I'm good at writing action in and out of bed, I'm not as good with pure romance. I now actively work on adding the little touches and glances that add up to tenderness.

That's one reason I sometimes write books where the only external conflict is the one between the hero and heroine. When you've been writing for decades, challenging yourself is the key to keeping your work interesting. If you're not fascinated and energized by your story, your reader won't be either.

Never stop pushing yourself. Do the thing that scares you because the book will be better for it. The books that follow will build on that progress.

Chapter Thirteen: Policing the Page

My husband Mike has been a cop since 1988, so I decided to interview him on how cops handle physical altercations.

These days, that can be a radioactive topic. Some cops have abused the system's tendency to give them the benefit of the doubt. People often assume that if a police officer kills someone, the victim had it coming. However, there are 1.2 million sworn officers in this county, and in any population that large, some will be dirty. Still, All Cops Aren't Bastards, Internet memes notwithstanding.

Yet sometimes, officers have no choice except to use deadly force. Others have made the wrong call or panicked and reacted with deadly force when they shouldn't have. Sometimes they're screwed whatever they do.

That tension makes police officers irresistible heroes -- and equally irresistible villains. Either way, writers need to know the reasoning and techniques behind what cops do, so that at the very least, their law enforcement characters are believable. These same principles can be used with characters who aren't police as well.

Police and Reaction Time

Action is always faster than reaction. In other words, someone can attack you faster than you can react. That's why police are trained to follow certain rules when dealing with subjects who may be armed and dangerous.

That's something you should keep in mind for *all* your protagonists. Anyone can be taken off-guard if they're not careful. That can be useful from a story standpoint, since readers love surprises -- including the nasty ones.

Keep Your Distance

Officers are taught to maintain a "reactionary gap" of twice arm's length between themselves and a suspect they're questioning. The cop should keep one hand on their weapon and an eye on the other person's hands, just in case they go for a gun. This training echoes that *Fight Science* YouTube video about watching your opponent's shoulders.

If the subject goes for a weapon, the officer must be ready to draw his own.

Justifiable Force

This has been a hot-button issue for years. It's gotten even hotter since the 2020 death of George Floyd and the Black Lives Matter protests that followed.

An officer *must* be able to justify the level of force used to make an arrest. *A badge is not a license to kill.* The officer must have good reason to believe the subject has done something illegal before they can make an arrest, much less escalate to deadly force.

Mike explained that the level of resistance the subject displays determines the level of force a cop can legally use. Officers are trained to use one level of force above what the subject displays. "The first thing we do is tell them what to do, and if they don't comply, that's an escalation."

If the officer tells the subject he's under arrest, and the subject says, "Fuck you," the cop can grab him, but *not* shoot him.

The levels of justifiable force vary from department to department. Some jurisdictions allow you to Taser a subject just for saying, "I'm not going to jail."

In the department where Mike works, the levels of force run like this:

Officer presence. The officer just being there is a level of force.

Verbal commands. They are a kind of force because they have the weight of the law behind them.

Empty hand controls. This means using bare hands to make an arrest. Empty hand controls can be *hard* or *soft*. Soft refers to grabbing and holding the suspect, even if you use holds that inflict pain, such as joint locks. Hard controls are blows with fists or feet.

Intermediate weapons. They include Tasers, pepper spray, and batons. (Though you must be damned careful with the baton, because it's easy to kill someone with a blow to the head. Even Tasers can kill, if you deploy them against an elderly suspect or someone with heart issues.)

Deadly force. Shooting the suspect.

You use empty hand controls if they verbally refuse to obey police orders, Mike said. If they get into a fighting stance, you are justified in going to an intermediate weapon. "You don't just get in a fist fight and see who wins. You are not a boxer," Mike explained. "Your job is to take them to jail if they're violating the law."

The officer does have options about whether to use force, he said. "If you lay hands on them and they fight to get away, you may use an intermediate weapon, or you may not. If they're actively trying to hurt you, you disengage and use an intermediate weapon."

If the subject is much bigger than you are, you

are also justified in going to intermediate weapons. "That's why we've had incidents of big football players getting Tased, because the alternative is to shoot him."

If a subject pulls a knife and they're within twenty-one feet and moving toward you, you can use deadly force. "Someone can cover twenty-one feet very quickly," Mike said. "You can Taser them, but you are also justified in using your gun."

However, shooting an attacker with a Taser is iffy at best, especially if they're running. A Taser shoots two barbs on unreeling fifteen-foot wires. A painful electrical jolt is fired through those wires that sends the body into agonizing muscle spasms. But since the probes function like tiny jumper cables, Tasers have drawbacks. If one probe doesn't embed in the skin -- getting caught in clothing or missing altogether -- there's no electrical circuit and you won't get that immobilizing shock.

Obviously, that becomes an even greater problem if the subject has a pistol, Mike said. "If you just get (a Taser probe into) the fabric of a jacket, there's no current, and you could get shot. So you want to use the weapon that you're sure will stop them -- a gun. You didn't make the decision to use deadly force: the subject dictated the force by his response to your commands."

On the other hand, if the subject pulls a knife and they're a football field away, you may draw your weapon, but you can't shoot, since they can't kill you at that distance. "But if they run toward you, you don't use a Taser, because you can easily miss. You must use deadly force then."

People sometimes suggest that police could shoot attackers in the arms or legs. That may work for the Lone Ranger, Mike said, but not in real life. Legs and arms are small targets that move fast, so you're likely to miss. Cops are instructed to aim for the middle of the chest, referred to as "center mass." It's a larger target with a lot of organs, and there's at least some possibility the person can survive if they get treatment.

Police Dogpiles

I asked Mike why a gang of cops sometimes pile on one person. He explained they do that because they're less likely to have to hurt the individual.

"If I'm alone and have to put him in an armbar (*a type of pain compliance hold*), I may end up applying more force than the joint can take, and he may be badly hurt. If three people grab you, they can subdue you without that risk. The quicker we can subdue him and get him in handcuffs, the less likely it is that someone will get hurt, including the suspect."

Handcuffing a subject can be tricky, he said. If the person is overweight, cuffing them with their hands behind their back while they're face down on the ground can cause suffocation. This is called positional asphyxiation because the chest can't expand enough to take a breath. That's what happened to Michael Brown, who died when officers piled on him and handcuffed his arms behind him. He was a big man, and one set of cuffs didn't give him enough room to breathe. "Sometimes we have to use two sets of cuffs attached to each other to make sure they can inhale," Mike said. "It's safer to cuff them sitting up."

The same thing can happen to fit people if they're handcuffed on a soft surface like a bed. (This is a peril you can use against your protagonist.)

Intermediate Weapons

I recommend that if you want to see how to use

these weapons or other police techniques, go to YouTube and do a search. Departments post training videos that demonstrate everything newbie officers need to know.

You'll also find other useful stuff, such as tours of police car interiors. Equipment has changed a lot since my husband was a patrolman in the 1990s, particularly when it comes to laptops in patrol cars. He's now a detective and doesn't transport suspects in his car, since it doesn't have the rear-seat cage to keep arrestees from attacking the officer. If he arrests someone, he has to call a patrol officer to transport them to jail.

Pepper Spray

Pepper spray uses a purified form of capsicum spray -- the same chemical that makes red peppers hot -- that causes eye and skin irritation. People shot with it choke, their eyes tear, and their mucus membranes burn until they lose interest in resisting arrest.

The problem with the spray is that not everyone is affected in the same way. It can also literally backfire. If there's any wind at all, you'll get a face full of your own spray, which could pose a deadly distraction.

The Portland, Oregon BLM protestors weaponized this effect by using leaf blowers to turn tear gas attacks back on police.

Batons

When my husband became a cop in 1988, he was issued a PR-24, which was a thick, heavy weapon with a handle jutting from the barrel at a ninety-degree angle. (PR-24s, which replaced nightsticks, are a version of an Okinawan martial arts weapon called a tonfa.)

On March 3, 1991, a gang of Los Angeles cops were videoed savagely beating Rodney King with PR-24s. This shocked the nation and triggered riots.

Departments abandoned the PR-24 in favor of telescoping Asp batons, which are much lighter and less likely to result in fatal injuries. You'll find many YouTube videos that demonstrate how batons can be used to subdue subjects.

Firearms

Mike said if you know someone is armed, you don't want to give them any incentive to draw their weapon. "Have your gun out or at least have your hand on your gun. Tell him to show his hands and draw on him if he does anything." The idea is to avoid having to fire, he said.

Like Mike, most officers go their entire careers without ever firing a shot at another person.

Another thing cops must avoid is being disarmed, even when they're wrestling with someone on the ground. Their duty belts are equipped with retention holsters designed to make it difficult for someone else to draw their weapon.

One television trope that really irritates Mike is a cop character giving up his weapon to save a hostage. Officers never, *ever* do that. It only provides the subject with another weapon and another hostage -- the cop himself, complete with weapons and a Kevlar vest.

If you're writing a police character, do a search on how to avoid being disarmed. While you're at it, look up "armbar," a technique officers use to handcuff people during a struggle.

Seeking Cover

If a subject opens fire on you, Mike said you should get behind cover, draw your weapon, call for backup, and return fire if you can do so without endangering bystanders.

Cover is anything you can get behind that will stop a bullet, such as a brick wall or a large tree. Things that won't stop a bullet are considered concealment -- that is, something that makes it harder for you to be seen and shot. Concealment includes car doors, a wooden door, or an interior wall. The only part of a car that provides actual cover is the engine block.

But in the end, Mike said there's only so much you can do. "Sometimes you can do everything right and get killed. Most often cops get killed because they failed to follow some of the basic precepts of keeping themselves protected."

One fatal mistake officers make is going to a domestic violence call and parking right outside the house. "What you should do is park next door and approach carefully so you can see what's going on. Don't stand in front of the door or window, because you can get shot."

Sometimes the situation doesn't lend itself to safety. In others, the officers simply forget their training. "But it's hard to stay on that edge," Mike said. "You get lazy or complacent, and it gets you killed."

High-Speed Chases

High-speed chases are so dangerous to the public that a lot of departments don't allow them in certain situations. Officers are required to radio dispatch and report when they begin a chase. Depending on the circumstances, the cop may be told to break off. (For example, you don't do a high-speed chase through a school zone at 2 PM in the afternoon.)

When I was working on *Arcane Heart* (2022), I used just that scenario. My heroine, Deputy Erica Harris, attempts to do a car stop on a speeder. She has no idea it's a setup for an assassination attempt. She narrowly avoids being shot and gives chase, but her sergeant (a bad guy) orders her to break off pursuit.

Mike told me that wouldn't happen.

"But it's 2 p.m. and they're heading into a school zone!" I argued.

"I don't care. If they shoot at a cop, we chase them until the wheels fall off." He explained that anyone crazy enough to shoot at an armed officer will shoot at civilians even faster.

Mike told me another problem with the scene was that Erica mishandled the high risk stop by approaching the car from the driver's side. (She almost gets run down by a second assassin making yet another attempt.)

For a minute there, I was afraid I'd have to trash my wonderful scene.

Then I realized Erica is a rookie, and it's believable she'd make that mistake. I had the sheriff show her bodycam and dash footage to the rest of the department to warn them they're being targeted.

My hero, Jake Nolan (with his link to his magical lion) has to watch the woman he loves come close to dying four times in ten minutes. (Two gunshots, one attempt to run her down, and a near collision with a school bus.)

One of the villainous cops says, "Too bad he missed," trying to goad Jake. It works. His lion spirit manifests, roaring, and Jake almost gets shot as every cop in the room draws on him. Which is why he and Erica break up at the midpoint.

Even if you screw up your research, you can still

turn it to your advantage.

Adrenaline Is Not Your Friend

Adrenaline can be a real problem in car chases because it causes tunnel vision ("Your Body On Adrenaline" video). You see only whatever is directly in front of you. As a result, you do *not* see the unsuspecting motorist driving into the intersection in front of you until you hit them at 90 miles an hour. And that's only one of the ways an adrenaline dump can affect perception.

Another problem is that when your body is flooded with adrenaline, higher brain function tends to go out the window. Blood flow is diverted to the arms and legs so you can fight or run, shortchanging brain functions like judgement and self-control. The result can be officers reacting with lethal force when they shouldn't.

Adrenaline also strengthens long-term memory, which is why people in an adrenaline dump often get Post Traumatic Stress Disorder.

Officers are taught tactical breathing to fight adrenaline effects. (Asken 2007) By breathing slowly and deeply, you can slow your heartbeat and keep higher brain function intact. (In the elevator scene, Jim uses tactical breathing to control a threatening PTSD flashback.)

Traffic Stops

Car stops can be one of the most dangerous things officers do. In 2019, eighty-nine officers were killed in the line of duty. Of those, six were attacked during traffic stops, and another sixteen were hit by cars. (Federal Bureau of Investigation, 2020)

However, there are techniques officers can use to

keep themselves safer.

For example, Mike said the best way to approach a car is from the passenger side. (Cops usually approach from the driver's side to ask for license and registration.) One reason to go to the passenger side is that drivers don't expect it, so you can see if they have weapons without exposing yourself.

That technique has the added benefit of ensuring you don't get hit by a car. Mike told me civilian drivers can get mesmerized by the flashing blue lights, resulting in their hitting officers.

Trouble arises when cops make so many traffic stops, they become routine. And routine can turn fatal fast. You can use that fact in your fiction to make life difficult for your protagonist -- and exciting for your readers.

* * *

Next, let's examine how to write magical fight scenes without breaking your readers' suspension of disbelief -- their willingness to believe the unbelievable.

Chapter Fourteen: Believable Magic

I love writing fight scenes in general, but I find magical combat the most fun to write. In my imagination, I watch fireballs and lightning crackle across a battlefield. The scent of magical ozone hangs in air that rings with the roar of dragons. They dive and soar overhead, the heavy flapping of their great wings booming. A werewolf battles a vampire under the full moon to the sounds of lupine snarls and curses. The smell of blood is so thick, it fills your mouth with the taste of copper.

The trick is to get readers to buy into your fantasy world. *We both know there's no such thing as vampires, but for the length of this story, believe in them with me.*

Putting Reality and Fantasy in Your Fictional Cuisinart.

There are a couple of ways to get readers to believe in the unbelievable. First, you can use sensory detail to ground your magic in familiar smells, sounds, and tastes. I once described a potion as having an acrid, burned-vegetable smell with hints of marijuana, star anise, and cinnamon.

You should also think about the logic of your world and how it would operate. How would it feel to work magic? What would a magic-using society be like? How would non-magical folks feel about those with Talent? What are the laws of this world like? How would people use magic to commit crimes? Really get into the details of the world you're constructing.

For example, in the Arcane Talents universe, magic requires grinding mental effort that gives you a headache and makes you feel exhausted and hung over. Giving spells a physical price adds believability. In real life, exhaustion can be triggered by activities as different as playing basketball and doing your taxes. It's logical that casting spells would be just as physically and mentally taxing.

Giving your magic rules and limits encourages readers to suspend disbelief. Technology makes that suspension a bit easier. My computer might as well be magic, considering how little I know about its mechanics. I do know I have to either plug it in or charge its battery to get it to work, but that's about it. I suspect that's why people are willing to believe in stuff like UFOs, astrology, and ghosts. In a world where your car talks to you, why not?

When I create a paranormal world like the Mageverse or the Arcane Talent universe, I spend a lot of time working out the magical system and imagining how it affects society. Each magical world you create will require different approaches. That, in turn, will keep your reader from getting bored.

For instance, Mageverse witches are far more powerful than those in the Arcane Talents world. That's because the Magekind draw their power from an alternate magical universe, since magic doesn't work on the Earth humans occupy. That's one reason humanity has no idea magic exists until the Magekind get outed by invading aliens.

In the Arcane Talents world, magic is a natural force like electromagnetism or gravity. That's why there are mystical lions, tigers, and bears -- they're bred to form bonds with humans who can meld their power with an animal's.

But for most Talents, the arts are the key to working magic. Bards sing their spells, Primos dance, Arcanists paint or draw, and Alchemists brew potions or cook. Since the public knows about magic, there are laws and Supreme Court rulings that govern its use. When my Talents cite court cases or Congressional bills that worry them, it makes the world seem more real.

How would magic affect American society at large? Since there's nothing the Pentagon won't turn into a weapon, I figured there would be a magical branch of the military, the Arcane Corps. Everyone in my Talent series with a big cat or bear Familiar is a military veteran. Considering how much damage a bulletproof lion could do, I figured the government wouldn't let just anybody bond with them, any more than the Air Force would let a civilian buy a fighter jet.

Even corporations use magic. Record companies sign Bard singers, and the pharmaceutical industry's star employees are Alchemists. Potions are for sale as everything from soft drinks to dementia drugs.

The radically different approaches to magic in the Mageverse and Arcane Talents let me come up with very different storylines.

Especially when it comes to fights.

Those two series aren't the only ones where I play with the mystical. One of my favorite bits of worldbuilding is found in *Infernal Desire* (2021), a novella which revolves around God, angels, and demons, as well as the children thereof. That book is chock full of weird fights, and I adored writing it.

Besides, what's not to love about a heroine with an evil tail?

Here's the fight that serves as *Infernal Desire's* inciting incident. This is a different kind of brawl with more humor than I usually do. Humor is one of those dopamine sources readers love, but it can be tricky to use in a fight scene. For one thing, jokes reduce tension, and you don't want that in combat. Too, it's hard to find anything funny in a battle to the death.

Still, you can get away with it if you strike the right tone.

Jokes and Mayhem.

Rafe

I materialized in an alley. The height of the buildings and the fire escapes attached to stained brick walls suggested a city. Didn't really matter where. God transported me where He wanted me to be. (*I always like to do a one-paragraph "establishing shot" to clue the reader in on where and when we are.*)

Now, why He'd use me instead of one of His angels was another question. It wasn't like I could ask. He did what He did, and I made the best of it. Just as I had since I was fifteen and my angelic father appeared to tell me it was time to fulfill God's plan for my life.

I'd been seriously tempted to tell "Papa" to fuck right off. But smartass though I was, I hadn't quite had the balls to tell those glowing eyes no. (*It's always a good idea to do the opposite of whatever the stereotype is. You'd expect someone with an angel for a father to be saintly and devout, so I made Rafe the opposite. That's a great way to intrigue the reader.*)

I moved down the alley making no sound at all, blessed armor rendering me soundless and invisible to all but the creatures I fought. Which was handy, because otherwise I'd have to worry about getting arrested. Cops don't like people walking around with enough weaponry to take out a SWAT team. (*By having Rafe drop the line about cops and SWAT teams, I reveal this is set on contemporary Earth. You need details like this, because otherwise readers have no idea where the story is happening.*)

A grating sound rumbled through the alley just ahead, followed by female screams so shrill with panic, the sound seemed to stab my eardrums like ice picks. (*Establishing stakes. Plus, nothing rachets up the tension like menacing sound effects without showing the creature that makes them.*)

My heart shot halfway up my throat and started a blasting beat. I'd killed or banished thousands of demons over the past four hundred years, but it was always terrifying. Bad memories seared my mind: huge teeth slicing into my body, claws ripping flesh. How many times had I bled on this job? No idea. I was getting so tired of this shit, but the demon -- whatever flavor of Diabol it was -- would kill an innocent if I didn't kill it first. So it was going to die.

Or I would. (*And there's Rafe's psychic wound. Also, profane and cynical or not, he's driven by the need to protect. This should hopefully engage the sympathies of the reader.*)

I rounded the corner and froze. *Madre de Dios.*

A Hell drake had cornered three scantily clad, cowering girls at the alley's dead end. Judging by the short skirts, the women had been clubbing, though I doubted Hellspawn was the hookup they'd had in mind. They screamed once more, again hitting that eardrum-puncturing pitch. I winced. (*When doing humor, effects like alliteration -- Hellspawn and hookup -- can add a hint of amusement to a situation that is otherwise grim. Rafe's humor tends toward dark anyway because that's the kind of life he lives. Now that I think about it, cynicism and sarcasm are probably the best way to use humor in a book with this much violence.)*

The drake was easily the size of a panel truck, a hunched beast with a wide, flat triangular head topped by branching horns. It had massive arms with inhumanly long four-fingered hands, tipped in curved talons. Four long tentacles whipped from its back, each positioned over one of its four powerful legs.

Fuck, this is going to be tricky. I raced forward and leaped into the air, my sword raised over my head. As I cleared its enormous body, I got a good look at the flat top of its head.

Oh, Hell, I thought as I fell, registering the demonic symbol that burned on its skull, the symbol of the master demon who commanded it. I'd memorized all the sigils of the major Diabol. This one meant the drake was a servant of Jargoth. Not just any demon, but a Lord of Hell. I... *Don't have time to worry about it.*

The drake jerked, sensing my presence, and my sword stroke missed, grazing the side of its head instead of cleaving it in two. I landed on its back, right between the whipping tentacles. "Run!" I bellowed at the women, chopping at the base of the nearest tentacle.

Make sure the fucker's too busy to chase them, Rafe. (This story is in alternating first person between hero and heroine. This can confuse the reader unless you give each character a distinctive voice.)

Zana

Oh, fuck the fucking fuck!

As Rafe started going *mano a diablo* with the Hell drake, I stepped off the roof's parapet and fell five stories. I landed with my knees bent, ignoring the teeth-rattling impact, and sprinted around the demon toward the three mortals. (*Which demonstrates nicely that Zana isn't human. This is what they mean by show, don't tell.*)

They took one look at my horns, tail, and claws, and screamed even louder. Ignoring the racket, I grabbed the nearest by the arm with one hand, seized the second with the other hand before she could bolt, and whipped my tail around the waist of the third. All three screeched and promptly tried to flee in different directions. Fortunately, nothing human can out-muscle a demon, though my tail protested the wrenching escape attempt with a burst of pain. (*Readers need to know how your characters look, but that can be tricky in first person narratives. You don't want your heroine saying something like "I have horns and long, bright red hair." Yet if readers are to imagine this half-demon character, I must give you some idea what she looks like. By having her mention her tail and horns in reference to how the other characters react to them, I can slip in the information in an organic way.*)

A quick psychic scan told me where the nearest girl lived, and I teleported all four of us.

They were still caterwauling when we

materialized. "Shut it!" I roared, casting a quick spell. They instantly fell silent, mouths hanging open, dazed and confused. Just the way I like my mortals. (*I love Zana. I don't get to write humor that often, since my stories tend to be a little grim. Fortunately, first person lends itself to sardonic commentary.*)

They wouldn't remember a damn thing after the nightclub they'd left just before attracting the drake's attention.

One girl's eyes widened as she registered my non-human face, but before she could screech again, I teleported back to the alley. Had to make sure Rafe hadn't gotten himself killed while my attention was diverted. The big idiot. (*She's deeply in love with Rafe. Unfortunately, he doesn't know she's alive. And if he finds out, he might kill her, halfbreed demon that she is.*)

I materialized back on the roof parapet and looked down.

Thank Gaia. There he was, leaping around the drake in his blessed black armor, holy sword blazing as he swung it in dizzying arcs.

I breathed a sigh of relief. I'd been afraid the demon would kill him while I was gone, but I'd known I had to get the Bimbettes clear. Otherwise, they'd have posed a lethal distraction for Rafe. With any luck, he'd assume the girls had escaped while his attention was diverted. His back had been to me when I'd teleported them, so I should be good. (*Note how little backstory I give. It would slow down the fast, snarky tone I'm going for.*)

I cast an invisibility spell and hunkered down on the parapet to indulge in my favorite pastime: watching Raphael Cazadero kick demon ass. Yes, I know I'm part demon. Shut up.

My tail poked me with its arrowhead tip. I ignored it. It tapped again, then wrapped around my left horn and gave it a vicious jerk.

"Fuck off!" I snarled, reaching up to untangle myself. I'd seen a movie once about an evil hand that tormented its owner. I know how the poor mortal felt. (*I adored writing Pointy. You do need to be careful with strange stuff like that, since it can get silly. Still, giving Pointy a separate personality and opinions was just plain fun.*)

Gripping Pointy firmly, I sat down on the parapet, swinging my clawed feet, trying to resist the impulse to wade in and help Rafe with his demon problem. I had no illusions on that score. He'd kill my ass the minute the drake went down. (*And there's her romantic conflict.*)

The monster might be able to give Rafe a run, but I'd have no chance at all against the Hunter. Which was why Pointy disapproved of my obsession with Tall, Blond and More or Less Angelic. It thought I was going to get us both killed. And it probably had a... OK, not a *point*, but whatever. (*"Tall, Blond and More or Less Angelic" is not one of my better lines. Sometimes jokes just don't work.*)

But Rafe was just so beautiful in battle. He didn't so much leap as flow, like a great wave, all muscular male power and inhuman grace.

I'd seen an angel fight my father once. That was more like watching a tornado grind toward you surrounded by airborne cows. (*When trying to create a semi-joke like that, I start with a base idea: how would it feel to watch an angel fight a demon? I thought the tornado image would get the idea across. How to capture the power of the tornado? Airborne cows do the job, while creating a humorous mental image. But again, be careful not to sound silly. I have crossed that line a few times.*)

Witnessing that battle had filled me with guilt and the horrible terror that when heaven's champion finished with Daddy Damned, I was next. (*Zana's psychic wound is that she considers herself evil, though she's not. She's a very lonely character, which is why she fell in love with Rafe after watching him fight her father. Yet because she's part demon herself, she tries to make sure he never finds out she's alive.*)

Rafe isn't like that. Yes, he's faster and stronger than any human -- I once saw him pick up a car and smash a demon like a cockroach. But underneath all the magic, beyond the flashes of wing you can almost see, there's a man. All tiger grace, inhuman speed and long, lean muscle, not to mention a sensuality you just don't see in angels. (*There's some repetition about Rafe's grace and power I should have cut.*)

He was doing real damage to the demon too, which is impressive in itself. Hell drakes are some of Lucifer's nastiest.

Acidic ichor splattered around the thing's severed limb as it pursued him, claws slashing, tentacles coiling, jaws snapping. Rafe ducked and pivoted aside, his sword licking out in a white-hot blur. Wedge Head roared in pain.

One of the drake's arms swung. I almost yelled a warning, but Rafe leaped skyward in a ten-foot bound that carried him away from the strike.

He was still airborne when a whipping tentacle batted him out of the air like a catnip mouse. Rafe slammed into the alley wall. I leapt to my feet. I'd have shouted in alarm, but Pointy slapped across my mouth, muffling the sound.

Rafe hit the ground and rolled, trying to dive clear, but a set of flashing claws caught him across the back. He screamed.

For a moment I saw the white shine of wings. Then he was on his feet, staggering away. A tentacle whipped around his waist, snatching him into the air so fast, the sword flew from his hand. The drake smashed him to the ground, then reared over him. Its massive wedge head dove down, burying teeth in his armored chest. He howled in agony.

Shit shitshitshit! (*When you want the reader to worry for your character, the character must worry first.*)

His blessed sword glowed where it lay against the alley wall. A plan burst full-bloom in my mind.

A bad plan, but a plan. (*Curiosity hook. That stuff is great for locking a reader inside your book.*)

Pointy coiled all the way around my head as if trying to restrain me from doing something stupid. I slashed my claws across it to make it let go. Pointy whipped clear and flailed. Eyes stinging at the pain from my self-inflicted wound, I flung myself through the air to plummet five stories. (*Half-demonic or not, her concern for Rafe demonstrates she's not evil. There's no better way to capture reader sympathy than to have your character fight to protect someone else.*)

The glove I conjured materialized around my hand just as I landed beside the blessed sword. I barely even registered the jolt of my bare feet hitting pavement.

Pointy flung blood in arcs of frantic protest as I snatched up the holy sword. (*When your protagonist is doing something suicidal or just unwise, it's good to have their friends speak up... or make frantic gestures in Pointy's case. Zana's got an imp buddy who also tells her she's crazy later in the book when she saves Rafe's life. The fact that her friends -- or body parts -- think this is a bad idea rachets up the tension. Do that every time you can.*)

I felt the roaring heat of the weapon even through the glove's protective armor. *Fuck, that hurts*! For moment I feared it was going to incinerate me, but I bounded toward the drake anyway. Wedgie hadn't noticed me, too busy trying to eat Rafe. Didn't even see me coming.

I smacked down on its flat, massive head, dug my toe claws into its knobby hide for balance, and rammed the sword's point into the center of Jargoth's glowing symbol.

Take *that*, Daddy, you sadistic fuck.

Wedgie's head whipped up, catapulting me

through the air just ahead of the holy blast wave from the blade. I landed halfway down the alley, hitting the pavement in a rolling tumble before bouncing to my feet again. Blinding light flashed as the sword did its work. When the light faded, the blade lay dark amid a pile of ash that swirled away as the wind took it.

A ragged yell jerked my head around. Rafe sprawled on the pavement, writhing in helpless agony.

Oh, Gaia's Leafy Green Tits! (*Zana and her mother worship a nature goddess called Gaia. And yes, I used the same name in* Master of Honor. *When you've written as many books as I have, you sometimes repeat them.*)

I knew better -- I really did -- but I hurried toward him anyway.

Staring blindly at the sky, he wheezed, as if to himself, "Well, that didn't go well at all." (*Understatement can be funny. It also works better for a character like Rafe than some cutesy eighties-style quip. He's also sliding into shock.*)

When I stepped up beside him, his eyes widened, and his entire body jolted as he took in my horns and claws. His lips peeled off his teeth. "Come to... finish me off?" His hand closed on his belt knife.

I took a hasty step back. "If I intended that, I wouldn't have killed that demon. I would've just let it eat you."

The hand drawing his knife froze, and he frowned

up at me. "That was you? When I felt... felt my sword..." He broke off.

I lifted my hand, displaying the palm of my glove. It was burned right through, showing my badly blistered palm. "What do you think?" (*She came way too close to incinerating herself, which is why Pointy was so upset.*)

Rafe's eyes widened. "That's one Hell of a... a glove." His expression twisted, somewhere between a grimace and a smile. "If you'll pardon... pardon the expression."

"It was." I flicked a glance at his chest and winced. The drake had bitten through his armor, leaving a ragged, bloody hole. The demon's inward-facing circle of teeth had left what looked like a bloody spoke pattern in his flesh. Not that deep -- the fucker must have been playing with him -- but the ragged red flesh was already beginning to darken, fat pustules forming. Shit, I didn't have much time to save his ass. I flashed his knife hand a glance, decided he wasn't going to try to stab me just yet, and sank to one knee at his side. "Look, the drake's venom..."

"... Is deadly," he finished between his teeth. He normally had no more accent than an American news anchor, but there was a soft Spanish sibilance to his words now. He must be in agony.

The thought wrung my heart like a wet rag. "I can save you."

He stared at me, his gaze beginning to go glassy. "In exchange... for... for my soul? No... no... thank you."

I huffed out a laugh. "You know better than that. I'm a succubus. We do sex, not souls. But I *can* do magic, and I did save your ungrateful ass before the drake could eat you."

Rafe licked dry lips. "I can... I can heal myself... if I can go home."

I made myself lift an eyebrow like I didn't give a shit. "So, go." (*She's scared of him, but she's even more scared* for *him. Otherwise, she never would have risked her life to save him. This should get the reader on her side, demon or not.*)

His lips moved as he began chanting a prayer, the Latin halting with pain. "*Oh Lord... if it be Your...Your will... save Your lowly servant...servant from the Wyrm's bite...*"

We looked at each other. He panted and stayed where he was. Damn, God was careless with His paladins.

Pissed me right off. "Can't help but notice you're still here," I pointed out. "And that wound's getting worse." The red flesh was darkening by the second. (*There is no better way to jack up the tension than a ticking clock counting down to disaster. That bite is going to kill him.*)

"I don't need... need... Hellspawn... help," he snarled.

"Too bad I'm the only volunteer." I slapped a palm in the center of his forehead.

He jerked. "Get your ha..."

I teleported us to my bubble, a pocket of time and

space protected from demons, Hell lords, angels and other undesirables. Rafe materialized spread-eagle in the healing pentagram. He took one look around, realized he was in the center of a working, and tried to leap to his feet. Thanks to the spell, his body refused to obey. Assuming it *could*, as badly as he was hurt. He swore at me in a torrent of gutter Spanish that made my brows climb.

I eyed him. "Does the Lord know you use language like that?"

* * *

When you've written as many books as I have, the best way to keep your work fresh is to construct new societies, new magic systems, and new combat techniques. I want readers to know that whenever they buy a book of mine, they're not going to be bored.

Chapter Fifteen: Swordplay

There's something romantic about a sword fight. Two men, meeting at dawn to duel over the honor -- or lack of same -- of a beautiful woman. Conflict, violence, sex, and romance, all wrapped up in a neat little package no writer can resist. Make it a *magical* sword, and you can have all kinds of fun.

But there's a lot more to fencing than two characters sticking each other with big shish kabobs. First, there's the question of the weapons themselves. People in prior eras were as endlessly inventive at engineering swords and knives as the Pentagon is at creating things that fly.

The design of swords changed a great deal over the centuries, depending on the fighting styles and technology of each period. During the Middle Ages, for example, swords were intended for use against armored knights. The design of the blade depended on the armor it was supposed to penetrate.

Armor ranged from boiled leather to chain mail to scale mail to full plate armor that covered a knight like a lobster shell. The armor worn by today's military has some of the same design features as historical armor, like a helmet and elbow and knee protectors. There's even a thick steel shock plate tucked into a pocket of the Kevlar vest to protect the heart.

Medieval armor was expensive to produce, which is one reason mounted knights were always nobles -- peasants couldn't afford the equipment or horses.

When you write a historical novel, check what kind of armor they used in that period, because styles did change depending on the weapon it was designed to protect against. For example, full plate armor suits were developed as a defense against crossbow fire. This, in turn, influenced the techniques people used in combat.

As armor got thicker, blades got longer and heavier. A medieval sword is basically a club with edges. A knight fought with a sword in one hand and a shield in the other. When knights fought on foot, they moved with the left side leading -- since the left hand held the shield while the right swung the sword around it to strike the opponent.

Once guns came into wide use, plate armor became useless. The musket balls of the time could punch through steel, so people quit wearing armor altogether. Too, equipping a large army with armor was expensive, and you couldn't march long distances in plate. (Though armored knights weren't as clumsy and clanking as movies would have you believe.)

However, the accuracy of pistols was initially poor, and the weapons were single shot. Reloading took time you might not have in combat. That's why swords remained in use for years -- you don't have to reload a sword, and they were a lot more reliable in close quarters.

Swords became much lighter during the Renaissance -- stabbing weapons rather than clubs, since they no longer had to penetrate armor. That resulted in a change of fighting style as the emphasis shifted to speed and skill more than the kind of brute strength an armored knight needed.

When civilians began to carry rapiers in the sixteenth century, they invented fighting techniques that could make interesting plot devices.

Rapiers were light weapons designed for one hand, which left the other free. A swordsman could fight with a dagger or second sword in his left hand, a technique called the Florentine style. He could also carry a small round shield called a buckler -- that's where the expression "swashbuckler" comes from -- or he could wrap his cloak around his forearm to block or entangle his opponent's blade.

Fighters developed elaborate techniques to block and attack with the blade alone. You can still see these skills in use in Olympic fencing today.

Fencing Terms

I'm going to describe fencing terms and positions here, but you may find it difficult to picture what I'm talking about. I'd suggest doing a search on YouTube, where you'll find a ton of videos about both Olympic fencing and historical rapier duels.

En Garde Position, also known as Guard -- This is the basic fighting stance of a swordsman. If you're right-handed, you stand with your right side toward your opponent. If left-handed, with the left side leading. This makes it harder for your antagonist to get a blade into anything vital; he's blocked by your arm if nothing else. The knees are bent slightly, with the toe of the leading foot pointed toward your opponent. The rear foot is at a 90-degree angle to the leading foot.

This is important, because that rear leg is the driving force behind attacks. (More on that later.) The weight is centered, and the torso is held straight even during attacks. This stance makes it harder for your opponent to knock you to the ground and kill you.

The sword is held with the palm upward and the thumb braced against one quillon (the cross bar of the sword). The arm is bent, with the elbow close to the ribs and the forearm parallel to the ground. During the attack, the arm extends, and the wrist turns to lever more force behind the thrust. The left arm is held out and back, elbow bent, then snaps out straight to add momentum during attacks.

Advance and Retreat -- The fencer moves forward by leading with their front foot, picking it up and moving it a few inches, then picking up their rear foot and moving that. (In retreating, the fighter moves the rear leg first, then the front foot.) It sounds awkward, but they can move surprisingly fast. It also allows the fighter to maintain balance, so they're vulnerable to being knocked off their feet and stabbed.

Lunge -- In the lunge, the fighter stands *en garde*. They lift their leading foot and use their back foot to drive forward in a kind of leap, landing with the forward leg bent. At the same time, they straighten their sword arm, powering the blade toward their opponent as their rear arm pumps out and down as a counterbalance. This lets the fencer cover a long distance quickly, hopefully smashing through their opponent's guard.

But if the attack misses, the fencer is extremely vulnerable because they're fully extended. They must quickly recover by pushing off on the leading leg and landing on the rear leg, while snapping their arms back into guard position. This allows them to parry and scuttle backward if necessary.

You must be ready to retreat in a hurry if an attack misses, because you're entirely too close to your opponent by then.

Parry -- knocking away your opponent's attack. You do this by striking their blade to knock it "off-line" so that it misses. It's best to parry with the lower third or "forte" of the blade, because that's where you have the most control.

Riposte -- To make an attack right after a parry, combining the two moves. You should always riposte immediately after your opponent's attack. Your objective is to get him before he gets you.

Those are the basics of a sword fight. There's a lot more terminology and techniques, of course, which you can pick up from YouTube and fencing manuals.

I wouldn't use a lot of technical terms, though, because your reader won't know what the heck you're talking about. Lunge, parry, riposte, advance, and retreat, are really all you need. Too much fencing jargon can confuse the reader.

Affairs of Honor

If you plan to write a dueling sequence, you will need to research the *Code Duello*, a set of rules of personal combat.

The Code evolved because when a bunch of young men wander around armed and half-drunk, they're going to fight. It was designed to keep bloodshed to a minimum and prevent vendettas that could destroy entire families. It was also one reason for the development of that elaborate etiquette men used with one another. When somebody might kill you over a minor slight, you become very, very polite.

Dueling was practiced from the 1500s until WWI, though by then, it was more of a fad among young German men to obtain a "dashing" dueling scar. They wore masks to protect the eyes, nose, and ears, leaving bare the cheeks they wanted scarred. (There are rumors that dueling persists today in dueling fraternities, though it's illegal as hell.)

Dueling originated as a form of judicial combat, since people believed you could win only with God's favor. Popes and kings outlawed it, but men kept dueling anyway, even if it meant they'd immediately have to flee the country. (I've also seen woodcuts in fencing manuals of women dueling men, with the man fighting from a waist-deep pit in the ground to make the fight fair.)

Men were very protective of their honor and reputation, because if you were dishonored, no one would do business with you, marry you, or even receive you in polite society. It was the male equivalent of a woman losing her virginity before marriage: he'd be ruined.

Speaking of which, impugning a woman's sexual honor would trigger an automatic challenge by her husband or male relatives. So would calling someone a liar. Striking another man would always trigger a challenge, or the one struck would be considered a coward and ruined.

After a challenge, a man would ask a friend or three to serve as his seconds. The duelists' seconds would negotiate to see if there was any way to avoid a fight, such as an apology. Some offenses, like a blow, could not be resolved by a mere verbal apology. According to the Irish version of the Code, you'd have to give the offended person a cane and allow him to strike you while you apologized. You could also exchange three shots and apologize afterward in lieu of the cane. (The pistols of the time weren't very accurate.) Accusations of cheating at cards, etc. were considered the same as striking someone. Any insult to a lady was a worse offense than if committed against her male relative.

It was the right of the challenged to decide if the fight would be with pistols or swords, unless the challenger swore he wasn't a swordsman, in which case pistols were used. The challenged chose the ground, the challenger chose how far apart they'd stand to fire, and the seconds decided the time of the duel and how many shots would be fired.

Challenges weren't supposed to be issued at night, unless one were leaving the area. I suspect this was to give challengers a chance to sober up and decide whether the insult was really worth risking death or having to flee the country.

The 1777 Irish Code Duello did not allow for deloping -- deliberately firing into the ground to avoid shooting your opponent -- on the grounds that the challenger should not have challenged over a non-existent insult, and the challenged should have offered an apology if he didn't intend to fight.

Americans might choose to ignore those rules, which is why Alexander Hamilton fired into the air and died when Aaron Burr shot him.

Dueling ended once people began using firearms that were so accurate, both duelists were likely to end up dead. That in turn meant the end of the Code Duello and the countless stupid deaths it caused.

Yet the craving for payback continues. That's why readers love to watch a protagonist finally get revenge for all the mayhem the villain has committed. Delivering that revenge in a well-constructed climax is the difference between a lifelong fan and a reader who'll never buy one of your books again.

Chapter Sixteen: Their Own Worst Enemy

Just as your first chapter makes the reader want to buy *that* book, the last chapter makes readers want to buy the *next* one.

If the climax disappoints, it may keep them from buying *any* of your books. And if they give the book a bad review, they may dissuade others from buying it too.

For me, the climax is the single hardest part of the book to write. As I've mentioned before, I usually end up stuck for at least a week, probably more, while I try to figure out the perfect climax.

Arcane Heart was particularly challenging, mostly because I violated one of my own rules for creating antagonists. I tried to pit a gang of corrupt cops against my magic-using good cops.

The book's Arcanist heroine, Erica Harris, can see magic and manipulate spells, though she's much less powerful than my Mageverse witches. The hero, Jake Nolan is a Feral -- someone who has a magical link with a lion, Clarence. His and the cat's combined magic lets them create a magical shell -- a manifestation -- around Jake with the lion's strength, speed, claws, and fangs.

The catch is that if either Jake or the cat dies, their spirits are fused in the surviving body. If the lion dies, he's trapped inside the man, and if the man dies, he's trapped in the cat. Either way, the human must learn to control the cat's animal instincts, which can drive him into a murderous rage.

If I'd stopped to really think about it, I'd have realized five cops are no match for a six-hundred-pound magical lion. Eventually the light did dawn about four chapters into the book, and I decided to replace the cops with a magic-using assassin.

But that left me with dangling bad-apple-cop plot threads I had to resolve somehow. I couldn't cut the crooked deputies completely because they helped escalate the romantic conflict. Without them, Jake and Erica wouldn't break up at the midpoint. But if I kept them, I still had to make them pay or I'd be left with an emotionally unsatisfying loose end.

The other issue was the pair of string-pulling politicians who engineered the whole mess. Virginia Laurel and President Roth had whipped the country into a national convulsion of anti-magic bigotry.

The whole point of a romance is a Happy Ever After. You can't have a HEA if you end up in a concentration camp.

Then there was the primary villain. Adrian Fleming is an Arcanist assassin who uses art to cast nasty spells. However, Arcane magic in the Talent universe isn't worth a damn in combat. Arcs are more like terrorist bombers. They can do a lot of damage, but only if they're able to make elaborate preparations ahead of time. Jake would kick Fleming's ass in any fight.

Now, I could have given Fleming a Feral partner, but I'd already done that in a previous book. When you're writing a series, you never want to repeat what you did before. As in fights, predictability is deadly.

I decided to explore how an Arcanist could get other people into doing his dirty work. In Fleming's case, he does gorgeous tattoos containing deadly spells that let him manipulate or even kill his victim. He couldn't use that on Jake and Erica, but he could use his tats to send killers after Erica.

Which still left the climax problem. I needed to send Jake up against another Feral, but not in the same way as in the previous book. The only candidate is Jake's best friend, Kurt Briggs. Briggs is inhabited by the spirit of his tiger, which died in the previous book.

Jake would have to fight Kurt.

Now, best friends battling to the death is a beloved trope in fiction because of the built-in internal and external conflicts. Fleming could cast a spell on Jake and set him against Kurt, thus forcing them all to relive the death of Jake's brother, Bobby Nolan.

(Kurt Briggs, Erica, Dave Frost, and Bobby and Jake Nolan were members of the same Arcane Corps team in Afghanistan. Bobby triggered a magical booby trap which drove his cat insane. He killed Dave, and Kurt had to shoot him. The experience has left them all traumatized, especially Jake and Erica, who was dating Bobby at the time.)

The scene takes place during a counterprotest Jake's mother organized against anti-magic bigots. This has the unintended consequence of providing Adrian with 6,000 potential hostages, between the anti-magic protestors, Jake's mother, her fellow Talents counter-protestors, and assorted cops.

Because I need to keep the cops busy -- otherwise they'd have Fleming ridiculously outnumbered -- the deputies must herd all the protestors and counter-protesters to safety. This works because it's the logical thing for them to do. The cops -- unlike Jake, Kurt, Erica and Genevieve -- have no magical abilities whatsoever, so they'd be vulnerable to whatever nasty magical boobytraps Fleming has planted.

A bigger problem is how would Fleming lure Jake into the spell he's created. Jake can see magic, so he's not going to voluntarily waltz into a boobytrap.

I decided to have the terrorist grab Jake's mother. As Fleming bellows mocking threats, Jake, Kurt, Erica and Genevieve approach the stone outcrop where the kidnapper is using Diane Nolan as bait.

Just to make the situation even more tricky, the terrorist is wearing a magical Spook Suit that renders him invisible. He's covered Jake's mother with a blanket spelled to do the same. Jake and company can only see the pair by closing their eyes and using their magical senses to detect the glow of the mystical energies Fleming's using.

"I'm starting to get bored," the Arc called.

With that, Jake's mother appeared out of thin air, blinking and dazed, as if he'd jerked the blanket off her. "Let me go, you bastard!" She jerked as if fighting an invisible hold.

Closing his eyes, Jake saw the glowing figure of a man standing with one arm wrapped around the smaller glowing figure that was Diane. The Arc's other hand held something pressed against her head. Probably a gun, also hidden by the Spook Suit's camouflage field.

"Let's get interesting." The Arcanist's voice, no longer distorted by the bullhorn -- he must have dropped it -- sounded amused, mocking. Jake didn't recognize it.

"Jake?" His mother sounded dazed, frightened.

"Shut up, bitch!" The kidnapper clubbed her hard with his gun hand. Diane fell with a cry, landing on her side at his feet.

Jake tensed in rage, his own and his cat's. (*This flashes a bright red warning sign at the reader. Jake's control over Clarence has been an issue throughout the book; Erica broke up with him over it at the midpoint. It needs to rear its head here too so they can fight through it. By the way, Jake and Clarence have conjured a manifestation. It surrounds Jake in a glowing lion shell with the teeth, claws, strength, and speed of the real animal.)*

His fury was all the hotter for the terror boiling under it. He ached to leap onto the outcrop and take the bastard out, but kidnapper and victim were twenty feet up and about five feet ahead. An impossible jump even for a flesh and blood lion the size of Clarence. If he missed...

The glowing figure planted a foot on the side of his mother's face, pinning her there as he aimed his invisible weapon down at her. Diane being Diane, she beat at his calf. "Get off... me... you jerk!"

The Arcanist laughed. And drew back a foot to kick her. "That's no way to..."

Oh, fuck this. Jake got a fix on his target's location, opened his eyes, and sprang. His human body could leap a hell of a long way carried by magical leonine muscle, but he'd never tried a jump that far. (*I needed to explain QUICKLY how he's able to leap that high. A big cat can only leap about half that distance vertically without a running start. By the way, the original sentence read: "Two hundred and ten pounds powered by magical leonine muscles designed for almost six hundred sailed through the air." You can see what a mess that line is. A bunch of clauses back-to-back are confusing. You don't want to force the reader to stop and decipher a line, especially during a fight scene. FIX IT. Especially in action sequences, you want short, clear sentences. Keep it under twenty words and get rid of compound phrases. Rewrite problematic sentences until you can read them aloud without stumbling. If you stumble, the reader will have to think about the line too long.)*

Glowing paws hit the lip of the outcrop, scrambled, almost lost their grip -- and caught. Roaring, Jake powered himself onto the stone in a furious surge. Snapping his eyes closed, he saw the Arcanist standing astride Diane.

Cursing, the kidnapper aimed the gun at him and emptied the clip as fast as he could pull the trigger. Bullets ricocheted off Jake's manifestation in an explosion of magical sparks. He lunged at the bastard, striking out with his claws, glowing jaws wide to display his armory of teeth. "You keep your fucking hands off my mother!"

With a defiant howl, the Arc leaped into a spectacular spinning kick aimed at his muzzle. Jake swung a forepaw, batting the Talent out of the air like a tennis ball. He went flying, hit a pine tree with a melon thump, and fell in a senseless heap. (*This bit is problematic as hell. You normally don't want to take out a villain this easily, because it risks an anticlimax. As I've said, fights with the main antagonist need to be at least ten pages long. In this case, though, there is no way Fleming could give Jake and Kurt a fight. Besides, what gets Jake in this mess is Fleming's spell, which he's about to land in. In retrospect, I think I still should have had Fleming put up more of a fight. Hopefully the battle that follows is spectacular enough that readers will forgive me.*)

Jake came down twisting to avoid Diane, who lay

coiled in a ball with both arms thrown over her head and hit the stone with all four legs apart. (*Damn, that's an ugly sentence. Should have broken out the part with Diana lying with both arms over her head. You don't want a big clause between the subject -- Jake -- and the predicate -- hitting the stone. I hate finding problematic lines after a book is published.*)

He had a moment to feel triumphant relief...

Until the magical trap sprang shut around him in an explosion of sparks and rotating sigils. He barely had time to think, *Oh shit!* (*Every time it appears the heroic couple is about to win, you need to have something go terribly, terribly wrong. The emotional whipsaw builds reader tension.*)

His brain seemed to detonate in a white-hot blast. Jake had never felt such blazing, frenzied rage, such a bloody craving to make someone pay. The bastard had dared touch Diane Nolan -- the single mother who'd worried and struggled and fought to give her sons a better life, only to be forced to bury one of them.

The magic-using shit had tried to *kill* Jake's mother.

He deserves to die.

Head low, the air around him vibrating with his snarl, Jake stalked toward the Arcanist, eyes closed to let him focus on his prey. The man stirred feebly, a bare twitch of his chin.

I'm going to bite the little prick's head right off his shoulders...

"Jake?" The voice was a hoarse croak, and he

opened his eyes to look around, lips rippling with his snarl.

The middle-aged woman lifted herself on her elbows, her face white everywhere it wasn't bruised and scraped. "Don't, Jake! He's unconscious. It would be murder."

"You can't tell me…" He broke off, and for a moment he recognized her through the bloody haze clouding his vision.

Until another wave of fury tore through him, ripping the moment of sanity away.

He roared. (*This moment is designed to freak readers out, because they'd know Jake would never get over killing his mother.*)

She jerked her gaze away and huddled submissively, her voice going high with anxiety. "You're under a spell! Like Bobby. Just like Bobby. Please, please, don't. I've lost one of you. I can't lose…"

That's Mom. I can't hurt Mom. He froze, shaking, trying to see her through the red-hot firestorm that hazed his vision with the need to rend and tear and kill. With the craving for blood.

Mom's blood. An icy bolt of horror jolted through his madness. *Get the fuck away before I hurt her. Start killing, won't be able to stop. Like Bobby.* (*He must fight the spell, or he isn't a hero. I also needed to show how the spell overwhelms him in his point of view. If it's just from the heroine's point of view, the reader may think he's weak. I had to show the effort he makes to protect his mother.*)

Somewhere on the ground below, a voice spoke, reverberating with magic. "Jake? What's going on?"

Kurt. Kurt's down there. Kurt can stop me.

Wheeling, he ran toward the end of the outcrop and threw himself over the edge. (*The act of going after Kurt is actually an act of self-sacrifice, rather than a loss of control. You want your protagonist to fight all the way down.*)

* * *

Her head felt as if it was about to topple off her shoulders if she made one wrong move, but Diane Nolan managed to crawl to the edge of the granite outcrop.

Twenty feet below, Jake's manifestation crouched, tail lashing, as he faced off with Erica, Genevieve, and Kurt's tiger.

Her son roared, the sound louder and more inhuman than she'd ever heard it. Whatever spell that bastard Arc had cast on her boy, it was bad. *No, damn it. Not again. I'm not losing you, too.*

Teeth gritted with effort, she reeled to her feet. And damn near blacked out again from the vicious pressure against her eyes. *Suck it up, Diane.* (*I wanted to show Jake's mom as being as courageous as her son, rather than merely a victim.*)

She needed to get down there, try to talk some sanity into her child. She began to hobble down the length of the rock. She was not looking forward to trying to climb down that slope.

Wait, where the hell was the kidnapper? The last thing she needed was for him to come after her. Diane closed her eyes and turned slowly, searching with her aural vision...

There he was, huddled on the ground at the foot of a tree, dead or unconscious. *He's lucky Jake didn't eat him.*

She started to turn away, only to realize he might regain consciousness and escape, especially given the Spook Suit. *Damned if that jerk's getting away after what he did to my son.* Diane hobbled over and bent to wrap her fingers in the fabric of his full-face mask, almost face-planting in the process. Bracing one hand against the tree, she finally dragged it off. It peeled off slowly, revealing a bleeding scalp wound. (*This plugs a plot hole. I needed to break the Spook Suit spell, or the bad cops won't be able to see him when they come looking for him. Norms can't see magical auras at all. Plus, I want to have Diane play a role in Fleming's capture. He'd have gotten away without her foresight.*)

As she straightened, his head appeared, looking decapitated. When she stepped away holding the mask, the spell broke and the entire man appeared, looking like an abandoned rag doll in black body armor. He was a big man -- dark haired and bearded, about forty, with the heavy muscularity of a boxer. His chest still rose and fell.

At least Jake didn't kill him. Not that he doesn't have it coming. Still, it would be better if he were alive to be questioned.

Shoving the mask into the back pocket of her

jeans, Diane turned to stagger along the line of the hill, searching for a way down.

With the sound of her son's menacing roars echoing in her ears, she knew she'd better hurry.

Then, dammit, I proceeded to forget about Diane. She doesn't show up in the aftermath of the fight. If you have a minor character in a climax, make damn sure you don't lose track of them. They need to at least make a reappearance. Jake doesn't even ask about her, and he damned well should have, given the last thing he remembers is almost killing her.

Losing track of plot threads is a big problem to watch out for, especially in the climax. You've been working on the book for months, and you're exhausted -- a big creative process like a novel chews up a huge amount of mental energy. Climaxes are also complex as hell, with a lot of moving parts and a lot of characters. Add a deadline on top of that, and the chances you'll lose track of details are high. It's probably a good idea to write yourself a list of everybody you need to come back to.

* * *

Erica latched onto Genevieve's arm and jerked her friend back away as the two glowing Ferals circled each other, muscles tense, heads low. She'd heard Jake roar a lot over the years, but he'd never sounded so thoroughly inhuman. Every time that savage, thundering sound raked her eardrums, it was all she could do not to flinch.

"Jake, you're under a spell," Kurt said, his magic amplifying his voice. "Remember what happened to Bobby? Remember what he did to Dave? I don't want to have to kill you to keep you from killing someone else, and you don't want to end up living in the tree house with Dave for the rest of your life. You finally have Erica. Don't screw that up." (*After his death, Dave was trapped in the body of his tiger, which now lives in Kurt's Briggs Feral Sanctuary. Jake will technically survive even if Kurt kills his human body, but he'd still lose his human life. He and Erica could never be together again. Since the reader is invested in the HEA, this rachets up the tension.*)

Genevieve leaned in and yelled into Erica's ear, fighting to be heard over the Ferals. "We've got to break that damned spell! We're going to have to get closer."

"You can't do it! It's going to have to be me. He won't kill me."

"Bobby killed Dave!"

"Bobby wasn't in love with Dave." She grabbed her shoulder mic and triggered it. "Sheriff Gable?"

"Any luck getting Nolan back under control?" He sounded as grim and desperate as she felt. "We're still trying to evacuate, but the crowd's on the verge of a wholesale panic."

"Warn them that if they run, they could trigger him to attack. Besides, Hussein Bolt couldn't outrun a manifested Feral. Walk slowly and calmly. If he charges, get down on the ground, cover your head with your arms and roll into a ball. Do not move. Do not make eye contact. Kurt will keep him from hurting you." *As long as Jake doesn't kill him.* "And I'm going to break the spell as soon as I can get close."

"How are you going to do that without getting mauled?"

"Magic." (*When you have a huge crowd of hostages, the protagonists' primary duty is to minimize the body count by getting them the heck out of the line of fire. Luckily, there are cops on the scene to do that here. Otherwise, one of the protagonists would have to get them to safety. That could give you an opportunity to separate the allies so the bad guys can attack them. The first question you should always ask is, "How can I make this worse?"*)

Jake lunged at Kurt again, and the glowing tiger leaped back, ducking a vicious slice of leonine claws. Roaring in frustration, the lion jolted after him, but the tiger danced away, probably hoping to exhaust Jake with a chase until his manifestation simply collapsed.

It might even work.

Erica licked lips gone dry with terror. She had to figure out how to break that spell, assuming she had the juice left after what she'd done with the Bards. Her head still throbbed like a kettledrum, but at least sheer terror had given her a second wind. (*The protagonist must work her butt off to win. Never make it easy. Easy creates no tension and no dopamine payoff.*)

Jake's back was to her now, and she edged closer, reaching for her Talent to examine his aura.

Oh fuck.

White burned so hot in his skull she could see the

frenzied heat through the golden blaze of his cat. Crimson sigils orbited him like moons around Jupiter. Deciphering them, she realized the spell was every bit as bad as she feared. It was designed to overwhelm the human half's centers of judgment and self-control while maddening the cat half. Probably the only reason it hadn't affected Diane too was that her Familiars were dogs.

Studying the spell, she took another step closer...

The lion's great head snapped around, glowing eyes narrowing in rage. His muscles tensed. Erica froze.

"Oh, fuck no!" Kurt charged, plowing into his friend. As Erica and Genevieve leapt away, the fight was on in earnest. (*I needed to give Kurt a reason to stop holding back. By having Jake almost go after her, I make clear how much danger she's in.*)

Damn it, the Arcanist bastard had known his business. Erica scanned the spell, but she could see no misshapen or badly spaced sigils.

Jake charged Kurt, who ducked aside, whipping out a paw to rake across his friend's glowing muzzle. Jake reared as Kurt leaped, and the two manifestations slammed together in an explosion of sparks. Wrapping their paws around each other, they ripped, clawing, fighting to puncture one another's magical shell and reach vulnerable flesh. (*You want to make any kind of fight like this as savage as possible. You can do this by using words like ripping, clawing and puncturing. Don't just rely on words like "cut" or "stabbed." Use words with punch. Use a thesaurus if you need inspiration.*)

Jake began to muscle Kurt backwards, and the tiger released him to bound away. Erica's heart sank. Kurt was moving more slowly, his manifestation no longer as bright, while Jake's lion shell burned as hot and moved as fast as ever. (*Jake is effectively the antagonist in this scene, which means that he needs the advantage in the fight with the protagonists. Here, that's Gen, Kurt, and Erica.*)

I'm running out of time. If he takes Kurt down, we're all screwed. Erica edged closer to the fighting pair, knowing she risked drawing Jake's lethal attention, yet desperate to see the spell more clearly. Every muscle tensed as she prepared to leap away if he turned toward her.

Then, at last, she saw it. One sigil wasn't quite as bright as the others. *There you are, you little bastard.* Not much of a weak point, true, but it was going to have to do. She started forward…

Jake's great maned head whipped toward her, gold eyes blazing, lips pulled back from fangs longer than her fingers. Erica froze, remembering the sight of Dave's lifeless body lying on the cave floor.

Leonine muscles tensed…

"Jake…" she whispered. Pleading.

His eyes widened as recognition flashed in their mad depths. His lips relaxed down off his teeth. "Eri…" (*Jake needs to fight the spell, or he'll look weak. For a moment, we think he's going to beat it, and then…*)

"*You're not touching her!*" Kurt landed on him in an

explosion of sparks, all four legs encircling Jake's torso as he dove for a grip on the back of the manifestation's maned neck, jaws wide, fangs glowing. (*I deliberately made the reader think it might be over, only to have Kurt blow it in an ironic reversal. Make the reader think they've won, then snatch it away.*)

Roaring, Jake twisted in a move no human could have matched, throwing himself to the ground and rolling. Sparks exploded as the cats twisted together, roaring in a deafening chorus, claws digging for purchase. Jake's rear paws raked the tiger's belly, leaving dim gashes in the manifestation where they penetrated.

Shit. Kurt's manifestation's definitely failing... (*Maintaining a magical manifestation is exhausting, and if the man and the cat run out of juice, it will collapse. Then Jake could tear Kurt apart. This fight, by the way, was inspired by hours of YouTube videos on fighting big cats.*)

Sensing the danger, Kurt released him and leaped away. Jake rolled to all four paws and dove for the tiger's throat. They tumbled as Kurt fought to escape, writhing and biting. But Jake got him pinned on his back, immobilizing him with fangs sinking into his throat. Kurt's shell darkened beneath the pressure of those glowing teeth...

The vulnerable sigil rotated into view. Erica raced toward the battling cats.

Insane, this was insane, but it was the only chance they had...

"Erica!" Genevieve's voice rang with helpless

terror for her husband, for Erica, for Jake himself, but Erica knew she couldn't stop. A thought flashed through her head: *If I don't have the juice to pull this off, he's going to kill me.* But she couldn't stop, or Kurt would die -- and Jake would be destroyed as surely as Bobby had been.

Thrusting out a hand, Erica sank her fingers into the dimmer sigil barely a foot from the lion's huge glowing head. And hit it with all her strength.

Nothing happened. (*This is Erica's black moment -- the moment when it looks like everything is lost as her magical blast fails to work. Your protagonist* must *fail at first to jack up the tension and increase the jeopardy.*)

Jake's eyes rolled toward her though he didn't let go of Kurt's throat. One forepaw released its grip on the tiger and lifted. *He's going to rake my legs open.*

Too fucking bad. She'd survive that. She wouldn't survive letting Kurt die. And neither would Jake. She shot her will toward the earth as Genevieve had taught her, fighting to draw power even without a spell circle. *More, I've got to have more...* (*You need a moment when the protagonist has the choice to run and survive or stay and risk everything. The decision to stay and possibly die is what makes them heroic.*)

A feminine hand landed on her shoulder, nails digging in hard. "Erica!" Gen cried. "Take mine!" (*Gen, the heroine from the previous book and a more powerful Arcanist, would logically play a role in this fight. The main actions need to be the heroic couple's, but Gen, like Kurt, needs to play a role. By the way, they'd actually practiced doing this earlier in the book. It won't seem as if it came out of nowhere. If you do come up with a trick like this late in the book, you need to foreshadow it earlier so the reader won't see it as a cheat.*)

Power blasted into her, a great blazing wave of it, nothing held in reserve, backed by all Genevieve's desperate love for her husband. Pain blazed through her, but Erica ignored the vicious burn as she grabbed her friend's magic like a drowning woman. Drinking it down, feeding her own into it, she blasted it into the sigil, backed by the raw force of her will, her furious determination not to lose either man.

The sigil blasted apart, vanishing in a cascade of sparks. Their joined magic burned right through the kidnapper's spell, splitting it wide, dissolving its sigils into glowing mist.

Jake's eyes widened. He froze, the grip of his jaws going slack. With a convulsive heave, Kurt drove his rear legs hard into the lion's belly, throwing him ten feet through the air. Leaping up, he drove a shoulder against Erica's hip, sending both women stumbling away.

Kurt whirled, planting himself between them and the lion. "Are you insane?" he shouted, without looking around at them. "Get the fuck back!"

Jake snarled, but the white blaze of psychotic rage burning in his head had dimmed. (*Erica can see violent emotions as part of her power. Though she's not as powerful as Gen, she's more sensitive to magic and emotions.*)

I've just got to snap him the rest of the way out of it. Ignoring the tiger's warning rumble, Erica headed toward Jake, sidestepping Kurt's lunge for her arm. Her gaze lowered, she sank to her knees until her head was lower than Jake's -- a gesture of submission. Slowly, she extended a shaking hand. (*This is the moment when she really demonstrates she's learned to trust Jake's control of his cat, even with overwhelming evidence that she shouldn't.*)

"Are you nuts?" Kurt snapped, starting toward her.

Jake snarled and tensed to spring...

* * *

I do a point of view shift here to show how hard Jake's fighting the spell. We need to see his black moment and his defeat of his demon. Experiencing it from his point of view makes it much more dramatic. In the first draft, I stayed in Erica's POV, and it just didn't work as well.

Rage leaped high in his mind again like another gust of burning hurricane wind. He growled at the glowing tiger, knowing only that it had hurt him, tried to kill him. Was getting too close to her.

"Jake!" the woman said, her low voice shaking with desperation. "Jake, please, don't!"

He knew that voice. Knew it mattered. The fury that had ripped through the cat's consciousness faded a little before the knowledge that she needed him. Almost enough to let him remember who she was. Who he was... (*We need to thoroughly establish just what Jake's up against in fighting this spell. This makes his battle to overcome it more gripping. He needs to show that even half out of his mind, his focus is on protecting Erica.*)

He stared at the slim, straight figure kneeling in the grass, her head lowered in submission. Slowly, she lifted one delicate hand, and he tensed, a warning growl vibrating through his manifestation.

She lifted her head. Dark eyes met his, deep and warm. And he knew her. *It's her... It's...* The thought spun away into confusion as he struggled to remember. (*By having him almost recognize her only to lose her again, I increase the tension and stakes.*)

A cool breeze blew into his face, carrying her scent -- rich, female. Familiar. He took a step closer, drinking in the taste of her on the wind. The rage that had bathed his consciousness in flame cooled again as he stared into those fathomless eyes. Stepped closer to that delicate, trembling hand. Drew in a deep breath.

Tasted fear. He tensed, his hackles rising.

"You're not going to hurt me." Despite the fear scent, her voice was steady. "You're not Bobby. Your control is better than that. Stronger than that. You won't hurt the people you love." A current of air teased him with her scent as the fear bled from it. (*This shows that she's overcome her distrust of him, that she's willing to make the ultimate leap of faith.*)

And he recognized her. Knew her. Almost knew her name...

"Come back to me, Jake. Come back."

He edged closer until his glowing nose touched those long fingers. They no longer shook.

"I love you, Jake." The words were low, clear. "Feel me. Know me. The way I know you."

Magic. Her magic. Rolling across his mind like a cool rain pouring over desert sand. His breathing slowed as her power danced along his. Calling him. (*She must help him win, proving that she deserves him -- and her HEA.*)

He wanted her. He didn't know why, but he knew that. Knew she was his. Knew he needed her. Had to have her.

"Erica..." The word rumbled, deep, hoarse. *Yes. Erica. It's Erica.* Memory bloomed through him -- the touch of her hand, silken on his skin, the intimate scent that lay behind one lovely ear, the taste of her nipples on his tongue, the salt and sex of her pussy...

"Yes," she breathed, exquisite eyes staring into his. "Jake. Jake, I love you. Come back to me. Please. I can't make it without you." Her voice vibrated with a note of pain that shook him to his core. "You're the best part of me."

Clarence moaned, a deep note of distress. (*Clarence himself has been MIA in this scene because of the spell, even though Jake is using his cat form. The spell had rendered them insane. Now we see Clarence again, so we know both he and Jake are back.*)

Yes, Jake thought. *She needs us.*

He released his manifestation. The glowing shell

vanished, leaving the man kneeling before his kneeling lover.

And Jake had his first sane thought since he'd leaped into the kidnapper's magic circle. *What the fuck just happened?*

The last thing he remembered was his mother, curled in a terrified ball at his feet as he fought his horrifying thirst for her blood.

Oh, Jesus, what did I do? He stared at Erica as she knelt before him. Proud, strong Erica, who never submitted to anyone. "What... what happened? Did I hurt you?" Jake rose, caught her by the shoulders and pulled her to her feet. Frantically, he scanned her body, breathed deep of her scent, searching for blood. But all she smelled of was... joy.

And relief, the kind of relief you feel when you almost die -- and don't.

A brilliant smile burst across her face like sunlight escaping storm clouds. "You didn't hurt me." She laid a trembling hand on his cheek. The love in her eyes shook him to his heart. "You'd never hurt me." (*The first draft of this scene lacked all this emotional interplay. He just comes out of it and kisses her. In the rewrite, I worked to increase the emotional intensity of the moment as much as I could. In a romance, the emotions are the engine of the story that drives the book.*)

"Good. Good. Oh, God, I love you!" Jake threw both arms around her, knowing only that he had to kiss her, had to anchor his consciousness in that hot, soft mouth. His mouth took hers, and to his inexpressible relief, she kissed him back, hot and frantic. As wild relief surged through him, he was distantly aware of the sound of applause and whistles from the watching audience of cops.

"Thank you, Jesus!" From the corner of one eye, he saw Kurt grab Genevieve and kiss her with the same desperate hunger he felt for Erica.

Where the hell had they come from?

Erica pulled back just enough to laugh softly against his mouth. "We're never going to live this down."

"I don't care," he gasped, and kissed her again.

* * *

You can see why this kind of scene is tricky to write. But if you can pull it off, the emotional punch will win readers and publishing contracts.

The question is, how do you know if you *haven't* pulled it off?

Chapter Seventeen: You Might Have an Anticlimax If...

Here's my version of one of comedian Jeff Foxworthy's bits, "You might be a redneck if..."

If the protagonist sits in the car while SWAT moves in... you've got an anticlimax. *The hero must be directly involved in taking the villain out.*

Your bad guy has been pounding on your protagonists for 100,000 words or so, and the reader really wants to watch them kick his butt. If the hero doesn't get to do that, the reader will be Very Pissed Off. And may never buy your books again.

Come up with a fight that runs at least ten pages -- twenty or more is preferable in a novel, though less is acceptable in a novella. You want to make sure the villains wish they'd never stolen the hero's Bible and kicked his dog.

If at the end of the fight, the protagonists don't have a scratch on them... you might have an anticlimax. *Make them bleed to show they earned their happy ending.*

Again, the reader must chew their fingernails over whether the protagonist is going to get killed. Or, as in *Arcane Heart*, lose everything that makes their lives worth living.

What's more, the climax must force the protagonist couple to confront their worst fears, as well as the thing that's keeping them apart. Ulf had to trust Cheryl to hold her own with the Hive scout. By the same token, Cheryl had to overcome her own fear of fighting the Hive, though she's never done anything like that before.

It took me weeks to design that fight to resolve all the book's conflicts. It's difficult to do, but if you can pull it off, your readers will adore you.

If you detonated an atomic bomb in chapter two… you might have an anticlimax. *The climax must be the biggest fight in the book.*

Again, sit down and make a list of the major fights in your book. (That's usually four in my case.) Figure out how they'll build. Maybe the first one is just a fistfight between the hero and a flunky. Then after that, the protagonists and two or three flunkies get in a gun flight. The hero is badly injured, one of the flunkies is killed, and the others run home to Daddy. Then in the third fight, the villain himself shows up with even more flunkies, and this time the couple must run for their lives.

For the final fight, hero and heroine are pinned down in a trailer park during a tornado, surrounded by a small army and the villain, who is holding the heroine's sister hostage. (I never did that, but you get the idea.)

Make it bigger and worse every time.

If you set something up and don't deliver it… you might have an anticlimax. *Keep your promises.*

Again, if you set readers up to expect that the villain will get their hands on the heroine and do Something Awful to her, that creep had better get their hands on the heroine. They're kept from doing Something Awful only by the heroine's courage and cleverness in arranging her escape with some self-sacrificial intervention by the hero. (Which results in near-fatal injuries to damn near everybody.)

Pay it off.

If the heroine wrings her hands while the hero fights for his life… you might have an anticlimax. *Get her involved.*

I can't stress this enough. I don't care if he's

Superman and she's five-foot-nothing and weighs ninety-eight pounds soaking wet. The heroine has *got* to fight for the man she loves. Otherwise, she's an annoying wuss who obviously doesn't deserve him.

Back in the 1970s, heroines were expected to squeal and faint whenever the villain and hero fought, but that was then, and this is the age of Wonder Woman. Go forth and Kick Some Ass.

It's in your best interest to avoid anticlimaxes like the plague. If you don't give the reader the delicious dopamine high they're looking for, they won't buy your next book.

If you do your job well, not only will they buy the next book, they'll go buy every previous book you've written, and you'll have a reader for life. Happy climaxes -- in both senses of the word -- are *the* way to get yourself on a reader's auto-buy list, regardless of genre.

Writing that kind of book takes planning, hard work and a willingness to endure frustration, because it's not easy. Sometimes you'll hit the climax and have absolutely no idea how to wrap all your conflicts up. You've got to be willing to gnaw on the problem for a week -- or a month -- until you come up with a solution.

Yes, I know that kind of block can be frustrating. How do you break through?

Beating Writer's Block

Here's what I do when I get a block -- and I've had one in every book I've ever written.

I talk out the problem with my husband, my critique partner, or my editor. Often just talking about the issue helps me break through. Just as often, though, my listener will tell me all about the solution that's staring me right in the face.

If that doesn't work, I go watch a loud, stupid superhero movie or something with a lot of explosions. Sometimes getting your mind off the problem gives ideas a chance to bubble to the surface.

Scientists think that creative thinking often happens at a subconscious level (Medlicott 2023), below conscious thought, where your brain connects ideas that don't seem connected. (Like vampires and the Knights of the Round Table.) Floating those ideas up into your conscious mind can be hard for your subconscious, especially if you're focused on a different solution.

Recently I've discovered that whenever I'm really blocked, I can take my phone for an hour-long walk and make a voice recording. I say anything that comes into my head, just talking through the problem. (I discussed some of this in the chapter on writing the elevator scene.) Nine times out of ten, I'll hear the solution come out of my own mouth without stopping off at my brain.

Exercise is great for creativity, probably because of the increased blood flow.

If I don't get anything -- and sometimes I don't -- it means the problem needs to cook in my subconscious a while longer. I go off and read or do art, then try again the next day. Eventually the idea will bubble up and I realize what to do.

Give it a try.

Just remember, never take the easy way out. The reader knows what the easy way out *is*, because they've seen it all before. You must show them something they haven't seen: an ending so surprising, so elegant yet wrenching, that it shoots them right into a happy dopamine haze.

To pull it off, you've got to be willing to make yourself, your protagonists, and your villain bleed, sweat and cry.

But I promise you, once you do pull it off, your reader won't be the only one in a happy dopamine haze. There's nothing more satisfying than finishing a book, which is why I've been doing it for thirty years over sixty or so novels, eBooks, and novellas.

May your writing career be just as long.

And if you're willing to put in the work, it can be. That means coming up with all the necessary internal and external conflicts for your protagonists and antagonists. Make damn sure you've got the right villain, then create a series of clashes in which they raise hell in your protagonists' lives.

Also, the antagonist must get theirs in the most spectacular climax you can arrange, thus forcing your protagonists to confront their inner demons in the process.

Finally, do the rewrites necessary to make the book as strong as it can be. Start submitting your novel to publishers. Or you can self-publish -- after first making sure you've hired a professional editor to ensure your book is as clean as possible. No matter how good you are, you can't really judge the quality of your own work. You need an editor to find all the mistakes you're too close to the book to catch.

If you don't know grammar or spelling as well as you think you do, you're not going to spot those mistakes. Readers *will* notice, however, and they're going to drop your book like it's hot. And publishers are not going to be impressed at all. Screw up the little stuff and they'll figure you can't pull off a strong book either.

The minute that final draft is done -- even before

you start looking for a publisher, in fact -- start thinking about the next novel. One book does not a writing career make. The fans you make with that first book are going to want the next one to read.

Besides, publishers don't want to publish one book. They want an author who will produce dozens of books over a long career. Writing book after book is the way you build that career.

It's the way I've built mine. I believe you can do it too.

Good luck -- and happy writing!

-- Angela Knight.

Dedication and Acknowledgment

For Michael, my knight in black Kevlar.

I'd like to thank my critique partner, Lynne Curry, for her invaluable input. Her advice helped me see where clarification was needed, and she pinpointed sections that needed a good pruning. And as always, I'd like to thank Margaret Riley, Changeling Press publisher, for being such a patient partner in making my writing guides available.

Anyone who thinks the pen is mightier than the sword never wrote a sword fight.

-- *Angela Knight*

References

- Asken, Dr. Michael. *The Adrenaline Dump: It's More than Just Breathing.* Police1, 15 Nov. 2011, police1.com/police-training/articles
- *ASP, Inc.* WikiPedia.org, wikipedia.org/wiki/ASP,_Inc.
- *Atomic Blonde.* Leitch, David [Director], Focus Features, 2017. [Film] imdb.com/title/tt2406566/
- Bergland, Christopher, 2012. *The Neuroscience of Imagination,* Psychology Today, 8 Feb. 2012, psychologytoday.com/us/
- *Code duello.* WikiPedia.org, wikipedia.org/wiki/Code_duello
- Cron, Lisa. Story Genius. Ten Speed Press, 2016.
- Cron, Lisa. Wired for Story. Ten Speed Press, 2012.
- *The Dark Knight.* Nolan, Christopher [Director], Warner Bros. Pictures, 2008 [Film] imdb.com/title/tt0468569/
- Federal Bureau of Investigation. *FBI Releases 2019 Statistics on Law Enforcement Officers Killed in the Line of Duty.* 4 May 2020, fbi.gov/news/
- FightSCIENCE. "1 Takes on 3 Like BOSS... TEACHES US Lessons in SELF DEFENCE." *YouTube,* youtube.com
- FightSmartTrav. "How to Win a Street Fight with Head Movement, Learn Simple (But Awesome) Street Fighting Techniques." *YouTube,* youtube.com/
- FightSmartTrav. "Fight Smart." *YouTube,* youtube.com/
- fightTIPS. *YouTube,* youtube.com
- FunkerTactical. "The Fred Mastro Handshake."

YouTube, youtube.com/

- FunkerTactical. "Fight Training Videos." *YouTube,* youtube.com/
- Knight, Angela. <u>Arcane Betrayal.</u> Changeling Press, 2023
- Knight, Angela. <u>Arcane Heart</u>. Changeling Press, 2022
- Knight, Angela. <u>Infernal Desire</u>. Changeling Press, 2021
- Knight, Angela. <u>Jane's Warlord</u>. Berkley, 2005
- Knight, Angela. <u>Master of Dragons</u>. Berkley, 2007
- Knight, Angela. <u>Master of Fate</u>. Changeling Press, 2019
- Knight, Angela. <u>Master of Fire</u>. Berkley Sensation, 2010
- Knight, Angela. <u>Master of Honor</u>. Changeling Press, 2020
- Knight, Angela. <u>Master of Magic</u>. Berkley Sensation, 2017
- Knight, Angela. <u>Master of Passion</u>. Changeling Press, 2019
- Knight, Angela. <u>Warrior</u>. Berkley, 2008
- Knight, Angela. <u>Wildcard</u>. Changeling Press, 2024
- Medlicott, Caragh. *The role of the subconscious mind in creativity.* <u>AYOA</u>, 27 Feb. 2023, ayoa.com/ourblog/
- *New Study Redefines How Dopamine Drives Learning, Memory, and Decision-Making.* <u>Cognifit</u>. Cognifit Blog, 26 Dec. 2024, cognifit.com/
- "Pepper Spray," WikiPedia.org, wikipedia.org/wiki/Pepper_spray
- "Baton (law enforcement)." WikiPedia.org. wikipedia.org/wiki/Baton.

- *Quantum of Solace.* Forster, Mark [Director], Distributed by Sony Pictures Releasing, 2008. [Film] imdb.com/title/tt0830515
- "Rodney King." WikiPedia.org, wikipedia.org/wiki/Rodney_King
- Shakespeare, William. The Tragedy of Hamlet, Prince of Denmark. *Folger Shakespeare Library,* folger.edu/ Accessed 7 Jan. 2024.
- Shakespeare, William. The Tragedy of Othello, The Moor of Venice. *Folger Shakespeare Library,* folger.edu/ Accessed 7 Jan. 2024.
- "Tonfa." WikiPedia.org. wikipedia.org/wiki/Tonfa
- darkscienceyt. "Your Body on Adrenaline." *YouTube,* youtube.com/

Angela Knight

New York Times best-selling author Angela Knight has written and published more than sixty novels, novellas, and ebooks, including the Mageverse and Merlin's Legacy series. With a career spanning more than two decades, she was awarded *Romantic Times Bookclub Magazine*'s Career Achievement award in Paranormal Romance, as well as two *Reviewers' Choice* awards for Best Erotic Romance and Best Werewolf Romance.

Angela is currently a writer, editor, and cover artist for Changeling Press LLC. She also teaches online writing courses. Besides her fiction work, Angela's writing career includes a decade as an award-winning South Carolina newspaper reporter. She lives in South Carolina with her husband, Michael, a thirty-plus year police veteran and detective with a local police department.

Angela at Changeling: changelingpress.com/angela-knight-a-26

Changeling Press LLC

Contemporary Action Adventure, Sci-Fi, Steampunk, Dark Fantasy, Urban Fantasy, Paranormal, and BDSM Romance available in e-book, audio, and print format at ChangelingPress.com – MC Romance, Werewolves, Vampires, Dragons, Shapeshifters and Horror -- Tales from the edge of your imagination.

Where can I get Changeling Press Books?

Changeling Press e-books are available at ChangelingPress.com, Amazon, Apple Books, Barnes & Noble, Kobo, Smashwords, and other online retailers, including Everand Subscription and Kobo Subscription Services. Print books are available at Amazon, Barnes and Noble, and by ISBN special order through your local bookstores.

www.ingramcontent.com/pod-product-compliance
Lightning Source LLC
Chambersburg PA
CBHW072137270326
41931CB00010B/1783